ULTIMATE GUIDE TO BREAKING INTO TECH INDUSTRY

Unlocking Opportunities, Mastering Skills, and Securing Your Dream Tech Career

By

JOSEPH STRONG

Copyright © 2024 **Joseph Strong**

No part of this book may be republished in any form or by any means, including photocopying, scanning, or otherwise without prior written permission to the copyright holder.

Table of Contents

THE TECH INDUSTRY **9**

    THREE THINGS THAT MAKE UP THE TECH WORLD 10

    WHAT IS THE TECH INDUSTRY? 11

    EXPLORING DIFFERENT SECTORS IN THE TECH INDUSTRY 12

    POSITIONING YOURSELF FOR THE TECH INDUSTRY 20

HAVING A TECH MINDSET **23**

    TECH MINDSET 23

    TYPES OF TECH MINDSET 24

    ENTRY LEVEL TECH MINDSET 25

GROWTH-LEVEL TECH MINDSET **41**

    HOW TO ACHIEVE THE GROWTH-LEVEL TECH MINDSET 42

    AREAS YOU NEED TO HAVE THE GROWTH-LEVEL TECH MINDSET 46

    HAVING A GROWTH PLAN & HOW TO PLAN YOUR GROWTH IN TECH 47

PROBLEM-SOLVING AND SCALE-LEVEL TECH MINDSET ... 51

    PROBLEM-SOLVING TECH MINDSET 51

    HOW TO HAVE A PROBLEM SOLVING MINDSET 52

    SCALE-LEVEL TECH MINDSET 54

    STRENGTH TO PERSEVERE IN THE TECH INDUSTRY 56

    HOW TO CULTIVATE ADAPTABLE AND RESILIENT MINDSET ON YOUR TECH JOURNEY? 56

FACTORS TO CONSIDER WHEN CHOOSING A TECH SKILL 61

    HOW TO ACQUIRE A TECH SKILL 61

    UNDERSTANDING YOUR PERSONALITY IN CHOOSING A TECH SKILL 62

    HOW TO USE YOUR PERSONALITY TYPE TO PICK A TECH SKILL AND LEARN . 65

CATEGORIZATION OF TECH SKILLS **71**

- DIFFERENT TYPES OF TECH SKILLS ... 71
- CORE TECH SKILLS ... 72
- SOFT TECH SKILLS ... 75
- ADMINISTRATIVE TECH SKILLS ... 79
- MARKETING TECH SKILLS ... 82

WAYS TO ACQUIRE A TECH SKILL? ... 85

- HOW TO DESIGN AND BUILD YOUR LEARNING CURVE ... 90
- HOW TO SUSTAIN YOUR PASSION TO LEARN AND FINISH SUCCESSFULLY .. 93
- KEYS TO FINISHING WHAT YOU STARTED IN TECH ... 95

NAVIGATING THE JOB MARKET ... 97

- BUILDING YOURSELF FOR THE TECH JOB MARKET ... 97
- INTRODUCTION TO FREELANCING? ... 103
- HOW TO GET FREELANCING GIGS/CONTRACT ... 105

MAXIMIZING SOCIAL MEDIA PLATFORMS AS A FREELANCER ... 113

- HOW TO CREATE AND POST CONTENT ON SOCIAL MEDIA PLATFORMS 113
- CREATING AN IN-DEMAND OFFER ... 115
- HOW DO YOU UNIQUELY POSITION YOURSELF? ... 115
- SOCIAL MEDIA CLIENT ACQUISITION FUNNEL ... 117

TECH MENTOR ... 125

- WHO IS A TECH MENTOR? ... 125
- WHY DO YOU NEED A MENTOR? ... 126
- TYPES OF MENTOR ... 129
- BENEFIT OF A TECH MENTOR ... 130
- HOW TO GET ACCESS TO MENTORS? ... 131
- HOW TO FOLLOW MENTORS ... 132

TECH ADVICE 133

MY TECH ADVICES FOR YOU 133

FUTURE PROOFING YOUR TECH CAREER 138

Introduction

In the 21st century, technology is considered the new 'oil' for valid reasons. The phrase "tech is the new oil" is often used to emphasize the economic and strategic importance of the technology sector with reference to the crucial role that 'crude oil' played in past economies after its discovery. Crude oil was essential for economic and industrial progress in the 20th century, and technology is now acknowledged as a key factor for economic development in the 21st century.

The IT industry acts as a stimulus for innovation, efficiency, and productivity in several areas. As much as I believe that technology is sometimes likened to the new oil, it is unarguably beyond a mere resource. This is because it provides a distinct opportunity and potent instrument that may ignite significant creativity and invention in individuals, regardless of their background or formal education.

The ever-changing tech industry with its vast learning opportunities allows individuals (who dedicate time to learn) to master different tech skills which help them to develop and produce tech solutions to solve real problems in our world. Technology provides a unique platform for individuals to demonstrate their creative and problem-solving skills, giving it that unequivocal edge over oil.

The tech industry's fast-paced and constantly changing environment in addition to readily available learning materials, allow people to gain new skills and expertise in many technical fields. It is now obvious in our world today that technology drives economic growth and provides equal learning opportunities which has changed the face of the 21st-century global economy.

The growth in the IT sector has led to a greater need for technical expertise. As a result, there has been a significant increase in both technology aficionados and those from non-tech backgrounds looking to take advantage of the industry's growth. Yet, it is worthy of note that a significant hurdle looms in the horizon for those seeking to enter or progress in the IT industry during this boom.

Some individuals encounter challenges while trying to enter the IT business due to a lack of necessary expertise or advice. Some individuals have the necessary talents but find it difficult to make money from them, facing challenges in accessing profitable possibilities in the technology industry.

Furthermore, some individuals who are already deeply involved in the technology sector struggle with expanding their operations and attaining significant outcomes.

This is where **"ULTIMATE GUIDE TO BREAKING INTO TECH INDUSTRY"** comes in handy as an extensive guide and a prolific handbook to give you the needed edge and set you on the path to success and significance in the tech world. It is a helpful resource for beginners entering the IT industry and supports experienced professionals transiting into this dynamic sector.

The book discusses the various complex issues individuals encounter, providing valuable insights, methods, and practical guidance to help readers succeed in the constantly changing world of technology. This book is designed to help beginners and experienced professionals transit into the IT industry and build successful careers in technology.

With this book, you will be able to step in and explore the IT industry beyond mere curiosity into a realm of creativity, advancement and results. In the world of technology, each hurdle represents a code awaiting decryption and every problem serves as a gateway to boundless opportunities.

Entering the tech field is not simply a process but your ***ticket to a future shaped by your creativity and the unending opportunities*** that awaits you. Join me in this transforming adventure as I guide you into the tech world and the IT business.

Upon finishing this book, you will be well prepared to make a significant impact in the field of technology. In Spite of its toughness and demands, technology can only be mastered by people who understand the art of hacking. I am here to disclose the essential secrets, ideas, mentality and endurance needed for this endeavor.

Once again, I welcome you on this exciting journey into tech, as I lead you through the crucial steps to achieving success in the ever-evolving field of technology.

CHAPTER 1

THE TECH INDUSTRY

The world of technology is like a bustling community where companies come together to craft, build, and share electronic wonders. When you think of the computers you use and other cool gadgets that catch your fancy as well as the software that makes it all tick, you suddenly realize it is a world of endless amazement.

It is not just about machines; it is about people creating, innovating and providing services that make our tech-filled lives possible. From designing sleek computers to developing cutting-edge software, the technology industry is a vibrant network of minds shaping the electronic landscape we navigate every day.

Take note of the word 'people' because tech is made up of people who bring their imagination and thoughts to reality. The most fundamental factor that cannot be neglected in the foundation of tech is 'People'. This is why, despite advancements in technology, machines and artificial intelligence will never be able to fully replace humans, as technology is a reflection of human ingenuity, imagination, and creativity. It is the result of individuals bringing their ideas to life, pushing the boundaries of what is possible.

Even as technology continues to advance with machines and AI, humans bring a unique essence to the table, which include intuition, emotion, and the ability to think beyond the confines of algorithms. While machines can perform incredible feats, they cannot replicate the nuanced brilliance of human thoughts. It is a testament to the irreplaceable role that people play in the foundation and evolution of technology.

Three Things That Make Up the Tech World

In my opinion, I believe the tech industry is made up of three components. Moreover, I do believe that a clear understanding of this standpoint will sponsor infinite creativity in us.

Surprisingly, these three components are People (humans), Imagination and Problem. These three sums up the word 'technology'. If I put it in form of an equation, this is what you have:

PEOPLE (HUMANS) + IMAGINATION + PROBLEM = TECHNOLOGY

Now that we know what the tech industry is made up of, we need to understand what the tech industry is, what goes on within it, how you can find your place, and make meaningful use of the tech industry to your advantage. I believe that is the reason you picked up this book in the first place and you will get just that and more.

Let's go!

What Is Tech Industry?

Tech industry is a vast realm filled with diverse job opportunities, often misunderstood by many who wrongly associate it solely with IT roles, technical support or even programming. Contrary to this popular misconception, the tech industry encompasses a multitude of positions that go beyond constant technical engagement.

There are roles where technical expertise is not the primary focus, allowing for a variety of skills and talents to thrive within the tech sector. To grasp the diversity within the tech industry, let us consider the medical field as an example. In the field of medicine, you have doctors but within that field, various specialists such as nurses, dentists, pharmacists, physicians, and occupational therapists contribute uniquely. Similarly, the tech industry hosts a myriad of roles.

Whether you are drawn to Tech Sales Engineering, programming, data analysis, QA testing, front-end development, full-stack development, UI/UX design, Solution

Engineering or like myself, Mobile App Development/Product Design, there is a place for everyone.

It is crucial to understand that the tech industry is not confined to specific technical roles alone; rather, it is an expansive space where diverse jobs co-exist. Similar to the various roles within the medical field, the tech industry accommodates professionals with a range of skills and responsibilities. From Tech Sales in a sub-industry to Solution Consulting and Solution Architecture. The possibilities are extensive.

The overarching message is that these roles are distinct, yet they fall under one umbrella known as the tech industry. Tech as an industry houses a multitude of jobs, each contributing uniquely to driving innovation, shaping the digital landscape, and influencing various aspects of modern life.

As you delve further into this book, you will discover detailed explanations about the tech industry and its core areas.

Exploring Different Sectors in the Tech Industry

Among the world's most diversified industries is the tech sector. Yet, when many people think of the tech industry they think of coding, Silicon Valley and astonishing company valuations. Others people also believe that the tech industry is male-dominated and soulless.

Both beliefs are wrong in this present age and time. I am a firm believer that in this age and time tech is not gender specific. Find your space and make an impact. Everyone has a space in the tech industry and if time and energy is invested, wonder will be rocked.

Tech is incredibly dynamic and that dynamism is what makes the tech industry so vast. It has seamlessly woven itself into the fabric of our daily lives to a point that our routine activities revolve around technology. Picture the tech world as an ever-changing puzzle composed of diverse pieces – different sectors that play pivotal roles in molding our lifestyle, work, and connections with the world.

With technology continuously advancing, it becomes crucial to delve into these sectors, each adding its distinct touch to the overall picture. By grasping these unique contributions, we unravel a complex tapestry of innovation and progress, providing us with a roadmap into the future of technology.

The tech industry is a fusion of hardware and software dependencies. These two components are intricately connected, often collaborating to craft the technological products and services that have become integral to our daily lives.

Before I show you a list of various sectors within the tech industry which have all been influenced by both software and hardware advancements, I need you to know something. RS Components discovered that there are more than 214 unicorn technology companies worldwide, each valued at over $1 billion. Consequently, the tech sector boasts of numerous sizable companies and this presents many opportunities for successful careers for anyone who cares to plunge into it.

Now here are some of the most influential sectors within the tech industry:

- ***Software Development:*** The design, development, testing, and upkeep of various software programs are all included in software development. It draws upon principles and techniques from computer science, engineering, and mathematical analysis, aiming to produce software that is efficient, reliable, and user-friendly. It is the backbone of the tech industry.
- **Hardware Manufacturing:** The hardware sector involves the design, production and distribution of physical technology components such as computer chips, processors and electronic devices. Innovations in hardware play a pivotal role in enhancing the capabilities of software applications.

- ***Artificial Intelligence and Machine Learning:*** Artificial Intelligence (AI) and Machine Learning (ML) represent groundbreaking fields in technology, fundamentally altering industries by granting computers the ability to learn and adapt without being explicitly programmed. This transformative capability enables these technologies to analyze vast datasets, recognize patterns and make informed decisions.
- ***Cyber Security:*** In our digital world, cybersecurity takes the center stage as the guardian of our systems and data. This crucial sector is all about keeping the bad people out – defending against cyber threats and attacks. Imagine cybersecurity experts as the digital superheroes tirelessly working to create strong shields against the constantly changing landscape of online threats. Their mission is to ensure the safety and security of our digital lives.
- ***Cloud Computing:*** Imagine a digital powerhouse that has changed the way we handle information—cloud computing. It is like having a virtual assistant for your data needs. Through the internet, this technology provides computing services including processing power and storage.

Whether you are a business or an Individual, it is like having your own personalized tech support, making sure your data is secure and accessible whenever you need it. Public and private cloud services have become the unsung heroes of modern tech seamlessly integrating into our digital lives.

- ***Biotechnology and Health Tech:*** Where technology meets healthcare, we get the dynamic duo of health tech and biotechnology. This field dives into innovative solutions e.g. telemedicine, wearable devices and genomic research, all aimed at boosting healthcare outcomes.
- Thanks to strides in medical technology, we are witnessing better diagnostics, treatments and overall patient care. It is like a healthcare revolution, blending the best of science and tech to make our well-being a top priority.
- ***Telecommunications:*** Think of the telecommunications sector as the heartbeat of global communication, making the world feel smaller. In 2021, the U.S. telecoms sector alone was valued at a whopping $278.8 billion, highlighting its economic significance.

Now at a global level, you have a staggering industry worth over $1 trillion. For anyone eyeing a career in the tech realm, telecommunications is a golden ticket. It is not just about the numbers; it is about connecting people, businesses and ideas across borders. The giants in this field like AT&T, Verizon Communications, Deutsche, Telekom, China Mobile, and Nippon Telegraph and Telephone, are the architects of our connected world with voluminous revenues as proof of their contributions.

- **E-commerce and FinTech:** In the digital realm, e-commerce and FinTech rewrite the rules, transforming how businesses and consumers engage in commerce and finance.

Picture this for a moment: your phone becomes your wallet, transactions are swift, secure and seamless—all thanks to FinTech. From online payments to digital banking and the game-changing block chain technology, it is a revolution unfolding with every click. Welcome to the future of commerce and finance where each tap is a step into the digital frontier.

Trends in the Tech Industry

Today's technology is developing quickly, allowing for quicker advancement and change, causing an acceleration of the rate of change. However, it is not only technology trends and emerging technologies that are evolving; a lot more has changed making IT experts come to realizing that their role will not stay the same in the contactless world tomorrow. Therefore, an IT professional will constantly be learning, unlearning, and relearning.

At this point, I must commend you as the reader of this book. It signifies the importance of staying up-to-date with emerging technologies and staying attuned to the latest trends. It is about being forward thinking, understanding the skills necessary not just for a secure job tomorrow but also learning how to navigate towards that future.

The trajectory of the tech industry sets the course for its future. Trends serve as concealed messages from the future to the present, signaling the need to prepare for upcoming opportunities. By delving into tech trends, you gain a profound insight, allowing you to predict roughly 80% of what lies ahead in the tech world.

For instance, consider the advent of Artificial Intelligence (AI). It heralds a shift toward 100% automation in various works and factories. Importantly, it is not about replacing humans but rather substituting tasks currently handled by AI-compatible jobs. Those who stand to benefit are the ones who learn to navigate the landscape – mastering the skills to use, operate, repair, and maintain AI systems. In this rapidly evolving tech realm, the advantage lies with those equipped to harness the power of emerging technologies.

The following are emerging technology trends you should watch for and make an attempt to get a good grasp of them:

1. Generative-AI
2. Computing Power
3. Extended Reality
4. Digital Trust
5. Genomics
6. New Energy Solutions
7. Robotic Process Automation (RPA)
8. Edge Computing
9. Virtual Reality and Augmented Reality
10. Blockchain

Absolutely, there is a vast array of emerging technologies beyond what is listed here. If I were in your shoes, I would wholeheartedly engage in research within the aforementioned tech areas. Moreover, exploring various other domains and strategically positioning yourself for the future would be a wise move.

In this ever-evolving technological landscape, staying curious, adaptable, and informed is the key to not just keeping up but staying ahead. It is a journey of continuous learning and positioning oneself to thrive amidst the exciting opportunities that the future holds.

Positioning Yourself for the Tech Industry

How can you position yourself for success in the expansive tech industry, given its vast and dynamic nature with numerous areas to explore?

- Identify a high-demand tech skill and gain mastery in that specific area.
- Acquire at least one trending tech skill, a skill poised to shape the future. When a tech trend first appears, it usually seems insignificant until it surprises everyone. For instance, consider Web3/ blockchain.
- Join a community that share innovations and talent for technology.
- Accept a communicator's role; master the art of speaking and writing about tech industry.
- Take advantage of the fact that the tech sector is always changing by continuing your education.
- Recognize your tech strengths and weaknesses and stick to them.

Understanding the future allows for preparation, preventing surprises. On the other hand, lack of preparation might spare you immediate surprise, but it can lead to regrets and the enduring pain of not being ready.

CHAPTER 2

HAVING A TECH MINDSET

In the previous chapter, I took you on a tour to see the vast landscape of tech—unveiling its various domains and offering a sneak peek into strategic maneuvers within the tech industry. As you go further, get ready to delve deeper into the intricate details that make this tech journey truly fascinating.

Chapter 1 was handcrafted for those with a burning desire to step into the tech arena but feeling a bit lost as well as those tech novices seeking a friendly guide through the technological cosmos. In this chapter, we will unravel even more layers of our tech exploration together.

Tech Mindset

The mind, bestowed upon us by God, is a potent instrument capable of fostering creativity, imagination and transformation. It is an important tool for generating outcomes and resolving challenges. The mind is the realm of thoughts- tangible entities residing within our imagination. The mind is the place that powers human's transformation

A Tech mindset is essentially a problem-solving, forward-thinking mindset that loves tackling real-life challenges using technology. It is the kind of mind that not only understands technological concepts but also excels in them. This mindset thrives on creativity, analytical thinking and adaptability, making it well suited for the ever-changing world of technology.

Someone with a Tech mindset is not just a user of technology; they have the ability to envision and implement tech solutions. Always eager to learn and adapt, this mindset embraces challenges with a problem-solving attitude in the digital and technological World.

The essence of a tech mindset lies in its problem solving capability. To possess this ability signifies the possession of a core aspect of a tech mind. However, it is important to acknowledge that there are foundational elements within the domain of a tech mindset that need to be established before one can be deemed to have a tech mindset. In other words, certain aspects of a tech mindset serve as the building blocks, paving the way for the development of a robust problem-solving aptitude.

Types of Tech Mindset

Here is a list of tech mindsets that can help you break into the tech world also known as the HAMMER MINDSET:

1. Entry-level Tech Mindset

2. Growth-level Tech Mindset
3. Problem-solving Tech Mindset
4. Scale-level Tech Mindset

The reason they are called the Hammer Mindset is that these mindsets are designed to break you into the tech world. After a careful study of the tech industry and my personal experience, I discovered I was applying these mindsets without even knowing it. When I first entered the tech field, I faced some challenging experiences that led me to discover these mindsets. I began applying them, and my results started speaking for themselves. I have not stopped applying them.

What I am about to explain to you is based on experience and a deep study and I will like you to pay close attention.

Entry Level Tech Mindset

I wish I knew earlier what I am about to share with you. I wish I had applied these lessons long before now because I would not have been frustrated and I would not have ended up trying to become a "TECH PROSTITUTE". I believe you might be wondering who a tech prostitute is.

Tech Prostitute is the person who is easily seduced by the tech field, wanting to dive into every area in the tech space and joining every startup that offers an opportunity. The individual delves deep into various fields without mastering any and one who knows a bit about many areas but has shallow knowledge in their own field.

It also refers to the person who jumps to try out every latest framework, programming language, etc. That is a tech prostitute. I was almost that kind of person, but thankfully, Iencountered a new mindset during my entry level into the tech industry. I am not saying you cannot have multiple tech skills. However, all I am saying is learn what needs to be learned but make sure you have one that you have mastered.

The following are the entry-level mindset you need to have to succeed in your journey into tech:

> **Entry Level Mindset 1: Do not see your tech skill as just a skill, see it as a career.**

The reason many people get frustrated in the tech field at the beginning is that when they start, they view their newly acquired skill as just a skill rather than a career or profession. When you perceive it merely as a skill, you might spend the first 6 months learning intensely to land your first job. However, after that you might spend the next 5 years stagnant, not growing and never progressing beyond the entry level.

Seeing it as just a skill leads to playing a short-term game. In today's world, skills are often portrayed as something you can learn in 3 months, 6 months or at best a year.

Thanks to online courses and boot camps! This portrayal may create frustration for many who, after completing these training programs, struggle to secure a job or land their first client—some may succeed, while others may not. The best way to maximize your tech skill is to perceive it as a career or a profession.

Having the mindset of viewing your tech skill as a professional career allows you to play the long-term game, make long-term learning investments and desire gradual growth over quick results. If you adopt the career mindset, your frustration level will be low but your growth and skill levels will be high and most importantly, your preparation level will be at its peak. Those who see their learning and career growth as a long-term journey tend to outsmart their peers because the tech world rewards experience, time, mastery and individuals who know how to perform the job even without professional-level experience.

When you start seeing your tech skill as a career, your focus shifts to growth and adding value. You become more concerned about becoming a person of value in the marketplace.

The tech field responds to individuals who bring value and not just skills alone. A skill-oriented mindset may lead you to work tirelessly without plans to develop systems and structures to scale up your workflow. In contrast, a career mindset works diligently and creates time for personal and career development.

A career mindset involves planning for growth and always aims to scale up because it recognizes that every time it scales up, there are new opportunities and challenges to conquer.

Opportunities will always look for people who decide to become professionals in their field. When you start adopting the mindset of a professional or career-oriented person, it naturally propels you to grow. In my discovery within the tech industry, one crucial thing I have found is that the state of your mind is very important—mindset is everything.

One thing you must avoid is the 'get rich quick' mindset especially as a newbie or someone transitioning from another professional career to tech. Do not view tech as a place where you can quickly make money. Of course, money is in tech but you have to work for it. You need to grow into a version of yourself that can generate the money you desire or need. My mentor always emphasizes that your growth is what matters in tech. If you want to make money quickly in tech, then grow quickly! Unfortunately, real growth takes time and energy.

While it is possible to make money quickly in tech, genuine growth takes time. When newbies are advised to take their time to grow, it should not be seen as someone slowing them down. On the contrary, when growth becomes your focus, money can be made quickly. Remember that financial success is often a byproduct of delivering value, innovation and hard work.

> ➢ **Entry Level Mindset: Learn With A Growth Mindset, Not A Money Mindset.**

Many people enter the tech industry to make money, which is not a bad thing. You may earn money, but you might become obsolete quickly. Making money in tech is not proof that you are growing. Let me share a short story.

A young man understood how to host and build websites using WordPress when there was not much tech activity in Nigeria. He made money; companies and businesses were always seeking his services. Regardless of the weather, people wanted a website on the internet with their company name. He knew the basics, used them to make money but he did not evolve. He stayed with what he knew, refusing to upgrade his skills and yet he had customers coming in. Of course, as humans, the moment they find someone more advanced, they will leave you.

Fast forward to 2023, he was no longer building websites. When asked why, he said it was not profitable. Then I ask myself, why is a lucrative skill like this no more profitable? The only reason he said it was not profitable is that the world outgrew his skill level. The world moved on, but he was still comfortable at his skill level just because it used to pay well.

If you focus on money alone, you will make money but you will not grow. However, if you focus on growth, you will make money, grow and be open to new opportunities. You experience more when you embrace opportunities. You experience more when you embrace opportunities.

Taking a cursory gaze at mindset, there are two basic types of mindset. They include a Growth mindset & Fixed mindset.

They are explained as follows:

Growth mindset: A growth mindset is the belief that your intelligence and abilities can be developed through dedication, hard work, and learning. You see great opportunities in every situation and you can improve as learn. You embrace effort, persist in the face of setbacks, and view failures as a natural part of the learning process.

When you begin learning a tech skill or you have just finished, let your mindset be a growth mindset – one that focuses more on growing and becoming more valuable in the tech market.

If you are a beginner entering the tech field, remove money from your mind; let growth be your focus. It reduces your frustration because, as a newbie, being money focused can lead to desperation. You might want to make money by all means, but the truth is you will be frustrated.

The proof that you have a growth mindset is that when you fail or go through frustration, you do not back down; you stand up and continue pushing forward, striving to achieve your results. A growth mindset keeps moving no matter what; it sees failure as a learning process. People who easily give up in tech after their first trial have a fixed mindset. Out of 1,000 people who decide to learn a tech skill today, only 300 will pay attention to their skill, and only 150 will continue because of the growth mindset they possess.

Fixed mindset: This mindset has a belief that all they know and have is all they need. They do not improve on what they have; they believe if they can deliver, they are cool. If they can do the job, they are alright. The mindset that leaves things the way they are never improving them to a higher level, People with a fixed mindset believe that their talents and abilities are predetermined and cannot be significantly developed.

Individuals with a fixed mindset may avoid challenges for fear of failure, as they believe that failure reflects negatively on their inherent abilities. They believe that talent alone determines success, leading to a reluctance to put in the effort required for growth and improvement.

How you know you have a fixed mindset is when you learn a skill today, and all you know is what you learned in that class. Two years down the line, you are still using the same pattern and level of knowledge in that skill.

> ➤ **Entry Level Mindset 3: Be Valuable to the tech marketplace**

When you step out into the marketplace, what sets you apart from others is the quality of the value you offer. The tech space responds to value, and every person who has made a significant impact in the tech industry such as Elon Musk, Mark Zuckerberg, Bill Gates and many more, have brought valuable contributions.

When you first embark on your tech journey, your primary focus should be on creating value. Ask yourself questions like, 'What can I do to enhance my skills?' and 'How far do I want to go with my skill?' The best way to gauge your value is by posing a real question to yourself, 'Can I employ myself with my current level of skill?' 'Is my skill valuable enough to meet my financial needs?'

As my friend would often say, "Are you worth $50k? Be sincere." He concludes with the statement, 'Become very good that company feel stupid not hiring you'. This encapsulates the essence of value. Make it your focus to become so valuable that anyone who sees your work is compelled to offer you a job.

Being valuable to the tech marketplace means ensuring that your skills contribute value to the tech industry. Every person reading this, especially newbies or those transitioning into tech, should focus on developing skills and knowledge that make them valuable contributors to the tech market. A person who brings value cannot be ignored; the same holds true for a techie with value – they cannot be overlooked.

> **Entry Level Mindset 4: Practice patience with the tech space**

The mother of destruction for newbies in tech is impatience. Impatience has destroyed many who just came into the tech industry. They come into tech today and want to still make money today. If you want to make it, accept the tech process.

You can be so good yet the door of the tech industry tells you to wait. When you see 'wait' it does not mean you get a reward; it only means it will add up when your time comes and tech will make it up to you according to your growth.

For instance, you just finished that 6 months boot camp, now you have a portfolio and then you apply for a job. Only to check your email and find out they rejected you. Well, do not feel bad. It is part of the tech process. It is meant to help you see what needs to be seen and know what needs to be known.

Tech process is so powerful that after you go through it, you become ready for your next opportunity. It might interest you to know that you will be rejected and you will feel bad but do not back out. Yes, never back out! Sometimes you post about your craft and surprisingly no one will come into your inbox or DM to ask for your services. This can go on for weeks, months and even a year.

However, you need to accept the tech process and remain patient as this opens the door for growth and most importantly, you will be able to learn from all your rejections and improve.

No matter how painful your first step to getting a job or 'gig' (as fondly called in the tech world), do not give up. The truth is you can get frustrated, you will be pained, you will apply for jobs and rejection will come but never let these things get to you.

There are some things you must have to keep doing and they are as follows

1. Be patient
2. Keep practicing -get deep in your craft
3. Never give up. If you give up, you lose big time!

From my experience, people who do not practice patience never make it big in tech. They might make money but not many make lasting impact. They might make money but they will not have enough value to keep them in the tech field for a long time. One time, my mentor in tech said **'Tech is a place of patience. If you stay true, it rewards you really well'.** I truly believe this now more than ever before.

I strongly believe that in entering the tech world as a newbie, patience must be your best friend. That is because tech is vast, learning takes time, setbacks are many and these are all part of the journey. To succeed, you must embrace challenges, feedback, and teamwork. Tech evolves fast, so stay curious. Projects might hit hurdles—be patient.

Celebrate small wins, balance innovation with stability and connect with the tech community. Have a long-term vision and remember, progress not perfection is the ultimate goal. Welcome to the tech adventure!

Lastly, in another context practicing patience in the tech space involves maintaining composure, adaptability and perseverance in the face of constant changes, challenges and uncertainties. It means acknowledging the dynamic nature of technology, embracing the learning curves associated with new tools and concepts, and navigating setbacks with a positive mindset.

Patience is essential when dealing with project delays, troubleshooting technical issues, collaborating with diverse teams and waiting for the adoption of emerging technologies. It also entails balancing the pursuit of innovation with the need for stability, fostering a long-term vision and approaching feedback and continuous learning with a patient and open-minded attitude.

Overall, practicing patience in the tech space is about cultivating resilience and staying focused on goals despite the fast-paced and evolving nature of the industry.

> **Entry Level Mindset 5: Imposter Syndrome**

I believe by now you must have gotten your first job or gig, or probably still trying to get your first gig. Whatever category you fall into, know this: in the beginning of your tech journey, when your first gig comes, the first thing that will happen to you is that you will not believe you can deliver. You will have a double mind and your thoughts will be such that you are trying to balance confidence with competence. By this, I mean that you know the job, but you will be scared of doing it. You might not even believe in yourself. This is known as *imposter syndrome.*

Imposter Syndrome refers to a psychological pattern where individuals doubt their own abilities and accomplishments, feeling like a fraud despite evidence of their competence. People experiencing imposter syndrome often believe that they do not deserve their success and fear being exposed as incompetent. This phenomenon is prevalent in various fields, including academia, business and the tech industry.

Common signs of imposter syndrome include downplaying achievements, attributing success to luck, feeling like a fake or undeserving of praise, and constantly fearing that others will discover your perceived inadequacies. Imposter syndrome can undermine confidence, hinder career advancement, and contribute to stress and burnout.

Imposter Syndrome in tech, especially for newbies, involves feeling inadequate due to high expectations, continuous learning, and comparison with peers, the pursuit of perfection, lack of experience, fear of failure and internalized notions of a "real" developer, designer, data analyst etc.

Systematic guide to overcoming the tech imposter syndrome

Overcoming this syndrome requires recognizing these feelings, seeking support and understanding that it is common in the industry. I had my own fair share of the imposter syndrome but I dealt with it using following steps:

1. **Just do it, do not mind the outcome, just do it**: What saved me when I got my first tech gig was that I just jumped on the job. Of course, I had my fears but I jumped right in with the mindset that I have to try it out. Eventually, I got positive results when I did. As a newbie or someone who wants to transition into tech, my advice is that you master the fundamentals of your craft then grow from there.

You do not need to know everything but know the basics before you jump into any job. Have a good understanding of your craft and then grow on the job. Your growth is always on the other side. The truth is that, the moment you start doing the work you will find out all the while that you could do it.

Therefore, stop belittling yourself today and jump right in. Many times your big tech breakthrough is in your big jump.

2. **Build Self Confidence:** I built self-confidence and kept telling myself I will learn on the job'. I kept telling myself 'I can design', 'I can code well', 'I can deliver', 'I am productive' and on and on. Learn to build confidence and one of the best ways to build confidence is by speaking to yourself regularly. Only you can speak to yourself and make yourself listen. Always have people around you who believe in you. Thank God for my mentor who believed in me no matter what happened.

3. **Recognize when imposter feelings arise:** Instead of dwelling on self-doubt, reframe negative thoughts. Focus on your accomplishments, skills and the progress you have made. Remind yourself that it's okay not to know everything and that learning is a continuous process.

4. **Seek Mentorship and Support:** Connect with mentors, colleagues or peers who can provide guidance and perspective. Sharing your concerns with others in the industry can help normalize the experience and offer valuable insights. Mentorship can provide a supportive environment for growth and learning.

5. **Set Realistic Goals and Celebrate Achievements:** Break down large tasks into smaller,

achievable goals. Celebrate your successes no matter how small and recognize that everyone, including experienced professionals, face challenges. Documenting and reflecting on your achievements can help build confidence and counteract imposter feelings.

Chapter 3

GROWTH-LEVEL TECH MINDSET

In chapter 2, we delve into one of the tech mindset known as the entry-level mindset, which is the foundational mindset. It prepares you for the next mindset, which is the growth mindset. The growth-level mindset serves as the building block after you enter the tech industry and pass through the entry level.

Growth-level mindset is the mindset that propels you to seek the advancement of your career. At this level, you no longer think like a beginner; instead, you focus on growth and advancement. The growth-level mindset is indicative of the fact that the state of your mind is proof of your growth.

However, never forget that the proof you have the growth-level mindset is your desire to upscale. You become more growth conscious as opposed to being focused on money or gigs. This is because in your growth, your tech journey becomes more manageable.

The growth-level tech mindset decorates your tech skill or career. It is the mindset of value, seeking advancement, and aiming to become the best in the field. You are not competing with anyone but yourself.

The growth-level tech mindset says, 'I have results in tech, but I am not just focusing on the outcomes; I am focusing on the process-the journey. While at the entry level, your default setting may be wanting results, money, gigs, and many other things, as you migrate into the realm of growth, everything changes.

Entry-level individuals may do anything to get results, which is understandable, but do not settle for results. Your focus should be on how far you are going in the tech industry, what you are getting out of it and what you are becoming.

At the growth-level tech mindset, you begin to look at things like your character, what you are becoming due to your results, your ability to communicate, teamwork and your ability to lead others.

How to Achieve the Growth-Level Tech Mindset

Achieving a Growth-Level Tech Mindset involves adopting certain practices and perspectives. Here is a guide to help you develop this mindset:

1. You must be intentional about your growth- Nothing and nobody grows without any form of intentionality. If you must grow, you must be intentional about it.

2. You must write your growth goal and be committed to it- This helps you define your intentions and know how much commitment is required to achieve them.
3. You must possess a profound self-awareness, comprehending your identity and discerning what resonates with you and what does not. Within this self-awareness lies your potential for growth. Many individuals venture into the tech field without delving into a thorough understanding of themselves.

   Some pursue skills that do not align with their personality. For instance, hearing about the lucrative nature of web development, they hastily jump into it without grasping the nuances of what web development truly entails.

   After about six months, frustration sets in—not because they lack the capacity to excel in web development, but primarily due to a lack of awareness. Awareness of their personality, strengths and weaknesses.
4. You must seek knowledge in areas that align with your self-awareness- When your pursuit of knowledge is rooted in an understanding of who you are, and then your growth in that domain becomes exponential. Knowledge acquired from a place of self-awareness

holds significant value and is more likely to be applied effectively. A tech enthusiast driven by knowledge will surpass peers who lack this awareness.

5. You must be consistent. Nothing beats consistency. Efforts accumulate over time into results when you are consistent.

6. Master discipline: everything rises and falls on discipline. Whatever you see working fine is standing on the structure of discipline. What does it mean to master the act of discipline? It simply means discipline has become your way of life, whether it is convenient or challenging for you, you decide to embrace it.

You decide to grow; you decide to add more energy to pursue that skill. To grow in tech, you must master discipline. You must take discipline as a part of the process and a major component of your success secrets in tech.

You can get motivated to start learning anything, but you need discipline to continue learning. Discipline is what feeds you and grows you in the tech field, not the number of tutorials or even the number of tech mentors you have.

Mastering discipline can mean setting aside specific times where you dedicate your energy to focus on your craft, grow and become proficient at it. It also means sustaining a staying power even when the odds are not in your favor.

If you want to grow quickly in the tech industry, you must be disciplined. If your desired result is to become an integral part of your tech journey, master discipline. Everything you are seeking in your tech career can be found in the discipline you might be avoiding.

7. Leveraging Mentors for Growth: Please, get a mentor. Mentors are growth stimulants. They can stimulate growth, whether you like it or not. When you are with mentors, they stretch your mind. A real mentor will influence your mind with thoughts that have the ability to stimulate growth.

   If you have a mentor in tech whom you have access to, someone you can text and call, and he or she can respond to you, then 90% of your growth is assured. A good tech mentor has a genuine desire for you to grow and achieve great things in tech. I will discuss this in detail as you read on and share on how to follow them.

8. Pursuing Knowledge in Tech: Inasmuch as you have access to mentors in tech, actively seek knowledge in tech. Learn to find knowledge and information by yourself; do not wait to be spoon-fed by a mentor. Your

growth will not happen if you rely solely on mentorship.

The knowledge or information you discover on your own stays with you for life. If you aspire to maintain a growth mindset, you must be a proactive seeker of knowledge.

Areas you need to have the Growth-Level Tech Mindset

There are very crucial areas you need to have the growth-level mindset and I will show you a few of them below. These areas include:

- Skill/Tech Character: This is an integral part of your growth. As many people begin to grow, they often forget about their character. This is why we encounter individuals who are highly skillful but exhibit traits of pride and arrogance, feeling they are on top of the world. A genuine growth-level mindset positively influences and shapes your character.
- Grow in your soft skills: One of the most important soft skills is the ability to be a tech leader and foster good teamwork. Invest time in developing these areas.
- Grow in your ability to sell yourself and your skills. Many people possess remarkable skills, yet they struggle because they do not know how to effectively

market themselves. Being good is like having a finished product, but without a marketplace and effective selling skills, your talents may go unnoticed. In the place of skills, learning and developing your selling skills is crucial.

- Grow in your communication ability: This area affects every field. Your growth and this area can change your life.

Having a Growth Plan & How to Plan Your Growth in Tech

A growth plan is a well-structured plan that makes sure you grow in any thing you do or any area you desire growth. A growth plan always leads you to somewhere, which is the desired result.

Here is a systematic guide on how to grow:

1. ***Setting Aside Time:*** Whether you are a newbie or a pro in the tech industry, setting aside time every 3 to 6 months to invest in the knowledge of your field is crucial.

Allocating time specifically for growth yields better results. You can choose to dedicate 2 weeks or more solely to investing in your personal and professional development.

When setting aside time, do you know there is a law in growth? It is called the law of 40 days. This law states that you can bring about a change in your life within 40 days. If you decide to focus on your craft for 40 consecutive days, especially after completing a boot camp and grasping the basics, you will become ten times better than those who attended the same boot camp with you.

If you are a professional reading this, dedicating 40 days to reducing your workload and immersing yourself in new information will significantly enhance your skills within that period in your career.

For newcomers in tech who have just completed a boot camp, here is what you can do in the 40 days:

First 10 Days:

Use the initial 10 days to recheck the basics and fundamentals. Aim for a deeper understanding of what you are doing. You might wonder if much can be achieved in 10 days – the answer is yes, if you set your mind to it. I did it and you can too.

Next 10 Days:

In the following 10 days, focus on cloning other people's works. Aim to clone 2 to 3 projects. Find a project that covers all the areas you need to learn and clone it.

Last 20 Days:

Allocate the remaining 20 days to building at least 3 projects of your choice. Ensure that the projects are achievable yet challenging enough to stretch your learning. However, here is a disclaimer: when you reach the last 20 days, you might find it beneficial to extend this period. As you progress, you will discover a lot that needs to be covered, and you will be inspired to grow and delve deeper. Remember, growth is achievable when you stretch your mind.

2. **Plan and attend tech events especially if it is even related to your field:** This helps you connect with others who can be instrumental in inspiring you and challenging you to do more or work harder.
3. **Stay up to date to the trends in your field:** Make the news your friend. Subscribe to newsletters, read up articles and blog posts on tech and make sure you find the news where you can. This is not to distract you but to help you keep up with your field so you do not get obsolete.

CHAPTER 4

PROBLEM-SOLVING AND SCALE-LEVEL TECH MINDSET

Problem-Solving Tech Mindset

No matter how skillful or up-to-date you are with the trends, if your skill and information cannot solve a problem, it is as good as not having it. Many people possess skills but struggle to apply them to solve problems in tech. Some dislike thinking through solutions in order to solve problems.

One common challenge beginners in tech face is expecting every problem to be the same and assuming that real-world problems will mirror those encountered during their boot camps. I also faced this challenge and it was frustrating and hindering my growth. What I learned was to open myself to the basics; they were tools given to me. My job is to understand the tools, how they operate, and be able to use them in a dynamic way to solve problems.

The key to problem-solving is dynamic thinking.

Never believe there is just one-way to achieve a task; there are multiple ways. Avoid having a fixed problem-solving ability; instead, think of different ways. You must be dynamic and flexible. The more dynamic you are, the easier it is to solve problems in tech. being dynamic means utilizing the basics and fundamentals to solve real-life problems. It also means not having a fixed mindset.

How to Have a Problem Solving Mindset

> - **Be a reader of books:** Books inspire you and open your eyes to new information. When you constantly consume new information, you increase your problem-solving ability. Because every time you read a book, you are thinking without knowing. For every time you read a book, you are solving a problem too without knowing it.

You may ask what problem? The problem is called ignorance. What should I read? Read books related to your field. Read books on leadership. Read books on communication. If you have enough information in your field, you can solve problems in your field.

But if you push it further by reading books on leadership, then you can not only solve problems in your field but you can lead others to solve problems and also teach others or conduct training for others to be able to solve that problem.

As long as you have information in your field and can lead, you will need to learn how to communicate your thoughts effectively. The greatest form of solving a problem is effective communication.

- **Believe that all problems have a solution and can be solved**: If you say it cannot be solved, it will not be solved. The first step to solving and developing a tech problem- solving ability is to believe you can solve the problem. Problems are there to push our thinking capacity so that we can birth solutions. Having a mindset that all problems can be solved is game changing. You may not have all the knowledge or experience yet to solve a problem is difficult. However, if you believe that you can, you will. Many times, the problems we face are unfamiliar, and it is our first time approaching such challenges.

When you face problems, do these things:

1. If you are unfamiliar with a problem, do research on that subject matter: What you do not know, you cannot solve. When you begin to study or research a problem, you will find answers.
2. Ask people who have experience in that field: That is why it's good to have mentors and friends who have experience in the field you're trying to solve a problem in.

3. Leverage the power of AI tools like ChatGPT. Many newcomers in tech feel they must solve problems on their own. While you can do this, it is important you know that when working on real-world projects, your priority becomes delivering results. AI tools assist us in solving problems faster. Those who use AI tools are not less capable in tech; they are simply being more productive.

Always see problems as opportunities to learn new things. Problems are the real teachers; they provide a wealth of experience. When problems become opportunities to learn and grow, you gain a permanent ability to solve them. Every time you solve a problem, you learn something new and you grow.

Scale-Level Tech Mindset

This is the highest form of mindset, the one that programs you for consistent growth.

Growth here does not just mean progressing slowly; it means growing exponentially. This mindset positions your mind for growth and results. In fact, anyone who consistently achieves results in the tech industry most likely has a scale mindset.

A scale-level tech mindset is the result of experience, time and energy, often accompanied by many failures. As a newbie, do not expect to adopt this mindset immediately. Allow experience and time to grant you access to this mindset. With a scale-level tech mindset, you can increase results without much effort. You know what steps to take to achieve multiple results at once.

A Scale-Level Tech Mindset is the mindset that enables individuals to increase their impact, efficiency, and effectiveness in the tech industry. It involves leveraging experience, learning from failures and continuously improving one's skills and processes.

People with a Scale-level Tech Mindset have a deep understanding of their field and know how to achieve significant results with minimal effort. They are adept at scaling their efforts, projects, and solutions to meet the demands of a dynamic and fast-paced tech environment.

Note: Scaling helps you become efficient and productive, resulting in growth. It increases your growth. In addition, never forget, scale-level is achieved over time. So for newbies, do not expect to have this mindset at the beginning of your tech career, but focus on developing it gradually. If you already have the tech mindset before entering the tech industry, you are already one-step ahead of everyone else entering the field at the same time as you.

Strength to Persevere In the Tech Industry

There are two more things I will like to talk about before closing this chapter and they involve having the strength to persevere in the tech industry. This strength encompasses emotional resilience, physical endurance, focus and discipline. As I often tell my students, tech demands dedication—you must learn to nourish it.

Even after adopting this mindset, there are certain challenges you will face. I faced them myself, and indeed, every newbie encounters them. There came a point where I felt like giving up. I was frustrated, and all I wanted to do was to remain idle. It took a toll on my emotional and mental well-being, especially when financial struggles arose. However, I found a way forward. Allow me to share with you the mindset that kept me going as you continue reading.

How to Cultivate Adaptable and Resilient Mindset on your Tech Journey?

Cultivating an adaptable and resilient mindset is crucial in navigating the challenges of the tech industry. It is your superpower to stay in the game and without this kind of mind, you will get frustrated and may probable quit.

Have you ever wondered why many start learning a tech skill today and by next 2 to 3 months they are backing down? Motivation is a great thing but a motivated and resilient person is always better. You need to learn to adapt. To adapt means readiness of mind to face whatever pain and frustration that comes with the tech skill you are learning and not run away from it.

In the beginning, tech will make you frustrated, you will experience frustration and if you are not careful because of the frustration, you will want to give up. The frustrations often encountered in tech stem from two main reasons.

Firstly, the process involves learning something new, which requires the brain to adapt to unfamiliar information. Secondly, attempting to grasp concepts too quickly can hinder true understanding. While rapid learning is possible, genuine mastery requires patience—a fundamental aspect of the learning process.

In addition, there is a reason we all got into tech. One of the reasons is to make money. I can tell you from experience, after learning or coming out of the boot camp, the next thing is to make money with your tech skill. Here is where many get to and give up because it looks like it is hard, or no job is available.

You would submit your CV, apply for jobs. Every morning, all I saw in my email was rejection emails from companies that I applied, which got me frustrated. Many people give up when they cannot market their skills in the first year.

As I told you before, that reward takes time and growth. The emotional frustration is there and it is real. One time I was so frustrated that I cried physically. I did an internship, yet I was not hired. These are the things sometimes you will experience- the pain, emotion, anxiety and even mental breakdown.

Another experience I had was the imposter syndrome. After all the pain and suffering, finally, a gig came from London. I was scared to do the job. In fact, I felt frustrated because I have experienced frustration and rejection so much that I had felt that I couldn't handle the job.

While rapid learning is possible, genuine mastery requires patience—a fundamental aspect of the learning process. You must be resilient in your tech skill, push like mad and do not relax. Even when tech is not paying, keep pushing and keep working on your skill. Tell yourself for every frustration I get, I will become better at my skill. Do not relax. The truth is you are not getting that job yet because to them, you are not good enough.

My advice for you is to become so good they feel stupid rejecting you. This was the advice my friend gave me. That advice made me vow to myself to go deep into my craft, take rejection as motivation to do better. If a girl rejects a boy or breaks up with him, the truth is some people turn that rejection into motivation to work on themselves to become a better version of themselves.

They work on making money. If you can turn your tech rejection and frustration into stepping stones to get better results, you will always be ahead of others. Actually, rejection is some people's final bus stop while to others; it is a stepping-stone to a greater height.

The more resilient you are, the more energy you generate to continue. If you continually experiencing frustration as a newbie in tech, especially financially, I advise, you to consider getting a side hustle.

There are two ways to get into tech: full-time and part-time. We will delve into this topic in more detail in another chapter, where you will learn how to successfully transition into tech without experiencing much frustration. I call it the *'Easy Tech Transition'*.

One thing you need to fix in your head is that in tech, learning never ends. Learning is very dynamic; it is not static. You should open your heart and mind to new ways of doing things and learn daily. Let something new in your skill get into your mind. The best way to excite our brain is with new information. How many of you are always excited to learn something new? Yes, count me in! That excitement does something to the brain.

Note: It is all about learning

- Learn to learn,
- Learn to unlearn old things that don't work,
- Learn to apply what you know,
- Learn to learn from others,
- Learn to plan your learning.
- Just keep learning. Learning keeps you going. The people who do well in any field are those who have decided to keep learning. Learning never ends; the day you stop learning, you start dying.

There are numerous benefit of constant learning as you move on inn your tech journey. Let me leave you with three (3) benefit of learning as you move on to the next chapter and they are as follows:

1. It make you grow in knowledge and information
2. It keeps your prepared
3. You will always be ahead of others

CHAPTER 5

FACTORS TO CONSIDER WHEN CHOOSING A TECH SKILL

In the previous chapter, discussed mindset, emphasizing its importance in preparing you for the tech industry. The foundation for anything lasting must begin in the mind. Everything is built twice: first mentally and then physically. Now that a tech mindset has been established, let us focus on building something tangible.

How to Acquire a Tech Skill

There are different ways to acquire a tech skill and we will discuss them extensively in this section:

- Through recommendations from professionals
- Personal research
- Following trends
- Attending tech clarity sessions and selecting based on personality, strengths, and weaknesses.

It is essential to consider all these factors when embarking on the journey of acquiring a tech skill to ensure a fulfilling and successful outcome. However, the most efficient way to acquire a tech skill is by studying your personality. I am not talking about passion alone; I am talking about studying yourself- who you are. Picking a tech skill without understanding who you are can lead to frustration.

Understanding your Personality in Choosing a Tech Skill

Personality encompasses the intangible aspects of your being that influence your outward appearance and actions. It encompasses your character, thought processes, emotions, attitudes, preferences and behaviors.

Personality dictates how you perceive and interact with the world around you, shaping your choices, responses, and mental resilience. It determines what resonates with you and what does not, guiding your inclinations and strengths while also highlighting areas of potential challenge.

Personality refers to the distinctive combination of psychological traits, patterns of thoughts, feelings, and behaviors that define an individual and tend to remain consistent over time and across various circumstances. It encompasses a broad spectrum of characteristics, including temperament, values, attitudes, beliefs, habits and interpersonal styles.

These traits are believed to arise from a blend of genetic predispositions, environmental factors, life experiences, and unique variations in how individuals process information and react to stimuli. Psychologists frequently examine personality to grasp individual distinctions, forecast behavior, and investigate elements influencing mental health and overall wellness. The Question is how does this relate to getting a tech skill?

If for instance, you possess an analytical thinking style, you excel at dissecting situations and devising solutions through logical processes and this trait is a fundamental aspect of your personality, when selecting a tech skill, opt for the ones that leverage your analytical abilities. Examples include software development, business analytics, and data science.

These skills inherently activate your analytical thinking prowess, making it easier for you to engage with the learning process. Given your predisposition as an analytical thinker, you naturally gravitate towards these domains, enhancing your proficiency and adaptability in the tech industry.

However, for individuals who naturally appreciate aesthetics have an eye for pleasing visuals and delight in harmonious color combinations, their affinity for aesthetics is embedded in their personality. They effortlessly discern good design and are quick to identify flaws in color schemes.

Tech fields that resonate with such individuals include UI/UX design, product design, motion graphics and front-end development. These areas align with their innate strengths, allowing them to leverage their natural inclination towards aesthetics to excel in creating visually appealing and user-friendly digital experiences. Their keen eye for design and appreciation of aesthetics serve as valuable assets enabling them to create captivating and engaging digital interfaces that resonate with users.

All I am trying to say is that you always find a tech skill that fits your personality. This makes the learning process easier and reduces frustration levels to zero because you are learning a skill that naturally aligns with your strengths.

NOTE: When choosing a tech skill, choose base on your personality, choose a high-income tech skill that resonates with your personality. Your personality and your potential financial reward must meet at a point. A good blend will validate your choice and fuel your resilience.

This brings us to another subject matter regarding personality, which is temperament. It is crucial to study your temperament and understand where your personality falls in terms of temperament. Personality is vital because of the emotional involvement that is required when you begin to learn a tech skill.

There are 4 kinds of personality type and they are the:

1. Choleric
2. Sanguine
3. Melancholic
4. Phlegmatic

Everyone who will learn a tech skill falls into any of these categories. Therefore, when picking a tech skill, prioritize selecting one based on your personality and temperament. This is crucial because many individuals enter the tech field without this understanding, leading them to constantly switch from one tech skill to another. This is not because the skill is inherently difficult or easy, but rather because they have not aligned it with their personality and temperament.

How to use your personality type to pick a tech skill and learn?

1. **The Phlegmatic**

The Strength of people with this personality, is that they are easy going and likable. Their weakness is inertia. If you are phlegmatic, the best way you learn a tech skill is by finding value in any tech skill you want to learn. Therefore, a phlegmatic person would want to go for a skill that has more value in the tech space because the truth is that not every skill has the same value. The moment a phlegmatic sees value in any tech skill, they can be one of the most tenacious sets of people. They are always value conscious.

Phlegmatic individuals, characterized by their calm, easygoing, and thoughtful demeanor, may be drawn to certain types of tech skills that align with their personality traits and preferences. Phlegmatic individuals often excel in roles that require patience, attention to detail, and logical problem solving; some of these are as follows

- Software Development,
- Database Management,
- Data Analysis,
- Systems Administration,
- Systems Administration etc.

There are many more but these are just a few of them listed above.

2. **The Choleric**

The strength of people with this personality type is that they take charge easily, and make decisions Quickly, I would say choleric are natural born leaders. If they are to choice a tech skill , it should be that which would make them be in charge of things, these type of skill are administrative and managerial in nature, if you are a choleric go for tech skills that allow you make choices for businesses and organizations because choleric are ambitious , and goal-oriented in nature.

They thrive in environments where they can take charge and drive results. If you are a choleric person, do not ignore the leader in you. Choleric excel in leadership roles, so they may be drawn to positions such as Chief Technology Officer (CTO), Director of Engineering or Team Lead. They thrive when they can set goals, make decisions and drive teams towards success.

Here are other tech skills that choleric can learn

- Project Management
- Data Science and Analytics
- Cybersecurity and Ethical Hacking
- Leadership in Technology
- Product management etc.

3. **The Sanguine**

They are often the life of every party but their weakness is lack of focus. If you are a sanguine and you want to pick a tech skill to learn and grow, turn your learning process into fun; make a game out of it. If it is not possible then give yourself a reward for increment in success or progress made per time.

The beauty about what I am sharing with you is that when you apply it, you will forever be thankful for the day you picked up this book. Add a bit of play in your learning curve.

They thrive in environments where they can interact with others, be creative and express themselves. In addition, Sanguine individuals are typically outgoing, social and enthusiastic. Here are some tech skills that sanguine individuals might be drawn to:

- User Experience (UX) Design
- Frontend Web Development
- Content Creation and Digital Media
- UI/UX Research and User Testing
- Social Media Management etc…

4. **The Melancholic**

These are life perfectionists. Paying attention to details is their strength. They tend to be so serious and because of that, they can achieve anything they pay attention to. A Melancholic person is a perfection freak but the problem is they are afraid to make mistakes.

They have a strong desire to go for perfection and for them learning any skill is not a problem, so long as they are paying attention to details. When picking or learning a tech skill they tend to focus on the joy of the details and potential for developing a level of mastery over the subject matter.

Another thing you need to know is that melancholic individuals tend to be introspective, detail-oriented and analytical. They excel in roles that require deep thinking, attention to detail, and precision because of their love for details.

Here are some tech skills that melancholic individuals might be inclined towards:

- Software Engineering,
- Technical Writing and Documentation,
- Database Administration
- Quality Assurance and Testing. Etc.

Every personality type has her strengths as well as their weaknesses when it comes to learning tech. You just need to tap into that strength in your personality and set yourself up for success.

Now you have an idea of personality and have possibly known your temperament type, let us move into the categorization of tech skills and how you can acquire them. Acquiring a tech skill can indeed be straightforward, but it can also become frustrating if the process is not approached correctly.

CHAPTER 6

CATEGORIZATION OF TECH SKILLS

Tech skills are skills for life and in reality; they are transferable skills that can be moved from one sector to another. You have an advantage when you have a tech skill. Some of the advantages include working from anywhere in the world, building a product of your own, you can solve global problems with a very good tech skill. Tech skills are not just skills for now; they are skills for the future. Personally, I see tech skills as wealth creation skills.

Different Types of Tech Skills

Before you acquire a tech skill, you need to know that there are different types of tech skills, which I have categorized here. They are:

- **Core Tech Skills**
- **Soft Tech Skills**
- **Administrative Tech Skills**
- **Marketing Tech Skills**

Acquiring a tech skill can indeed be straightforward, but it can also become frustrating if the process is not approached correctly. It is not just about selecting a skill; it is about how you go about the acquisition process and your mindset throughout. Many individuals have learned various tech skills only to find themselves not using any of them, feeling frustrated or losing passion after acquisition due to the process itself.

Currently, there are individuals looking to transition into the tech industry but are unsure of which skill to choose. This is where I come in to offer guidance. Others may already possess a tech skill but feel unfulfilled in that area, leading to a loss of passion despite knowing they should be in tech. Then there are those who want to choose a tech skill based on trends, which is not necessarily a bad approach, but what if those trends do not align with their interests or strengths?

Core Tech Skills

Core tech skills are skills upon which other tech skills are built. Core tech skills refer to fundamental knowledge and areas that are essential for success in various technology-related fields.

These skills serve as the foundation upon which more specialized or advanced skills can be built. These are not just skills; they give birth to other skills. The advantage of learning and having a core tech skill is that you are always valuable in every tech transition and era.

This is so because the new tech era or phase is still built on this tech skill(s) and all you have to do is to use your fundamental skills and align to the new ways of doing things. The beauty of this tech skill is that it never gets old. One thing you can be sure of is that it is the foundation and it must be solid in every part of any system, which makes it valuable.

Having a core tech skill and being good at it means you can never go broke having a core tech skill in possession.

Here are the examples of core skills,

- Programming: This is your ability to program in at list one programming language, it is very important for many tech roles. Programming is one skill that is transferable from one phase of tech to another. Not all tech skills are transferable as tech advances some will die a natural death, due to things like Ai , Automated systems, advanced technology, but programming has played a very huge role in the tech industry, learning programming at least one language and be go at it, examples of programming languages Python, Java, JavaScript, C++, and SQL and many more.
- Data Structures and Algorithms: I like saying this and I found out it was true. Actually, tech is data based. We are either moving data from one place to another or

generating data. If we are not generating data, we are also displaying data.

- Database Management
- Web Development
- Networking and Security
- Operating Systems
- Version Control Systems
- Problem-Solving and Critical Thinking
- UI/UX
- Cloud Computing

By the way, this is not exhaustive of all the core tech skills that there is. There are many more and I encourage you to do your research. However, it is worthy of note that for you to identify a core tech skill, you will know a core tech skill in the following ways:

- How long it should take you to learn (at least 6 months to 1 year)
- How demanding it is in the marketplace
- The skill must be transferable
- Check job boards or platforms: This is very important. Job board will always show you skills that are top ranked and in high demand.

I will encourage you to do research on skills that have always been in high demand in every tech era or phase.

Soft Tech Skills

I call this skill the invisible skills but it is a very important skill. They are mostly interpersonal or non-technical skills, which are essential for success in the tech industry.

Soft skills are important for effective collaboration, communication and problem solving. Now many techies ignore this skill but this is one of the most sought after skills because as good as your tech skill is, if you cannot work with others using that tech skill then you might be tagged as unproductive.

If you are a newbie reading this, get a soft skill. It would give you an edge in any place you work. Soft tech skills are largely what we use to work with our fellow humans. Actually, it involves our emotions. Companies and organizations are constantly looking for people who are skillful enough but can still work with a team towards achieving a common goal.

This is what is called collaboration. It requires that one should adapt to the company culture and environment. They include how you interact with colleagues, how you solve problems and how you manage your work. Just the way you would take your core skill seriously, take this as well.

Soft skills relate to how you work. Soft skills include interpersonal (people) skills, communication skills, listening skills, time management, problem solving, leadership and empathy, among others. They are among the top skills employers seek in the candidates they hire because soft skills are important for just about every job.

Here are List of some soft tech skill every techie should have:

1. **Communication:** Clear and effective communication is needed for conveying ideas, discussing technical concepts and collaborating with team members. Tech professionals need to communicate clearly both verbally and non-verbally, whether in meetings, emails, documentation, or presentations.

   Do not joke with communication because it is one very essential skill. No matter how skillful you are, communication is a major key to effectiveness. If you can communicate effectively, you will excel in any field. If you want to increase your income, become a better communicator.

2. **Collaboration:** Tech projects would always involve teamwork. Therefore, the ability to collaborate effectively is crucial. This includes being able to listen to others, share ideas, provide constructive feedback

and work towards common goals. Collaboration skills also involve respecting diverse perspectives and fostering a positive team environment.

3. **Adaptability:** The tech field is one that is very dynamic and always evolving. The tech industry is constantly evolving, with new technologies, tools and methodologies emerging regularly. You must be up-to-date, adaptable, flexible, and willing to learn new skills, adapt to changes and embrace innovation. The proof you are adaptive is that you are always open to positive tech change, and willing to step out of your comfort zone to flow with the tide.

4. **Problem solving:** This is the skill that companies tend to focus on when hiring techies. If you can solve problems for them, then you are of valuable to them. Complex problems and challenges are regular things and so strong problem-solving skills are essential.
Problem solvers are good at analyzing issues, identifying root causes and devising effective solutions. Problem-solving skills also include critical thinking, creativity and the ability to approach problems from different perspectives.

5. **Time Management:** Time is everything. Everything is time bound, especially in tech when it comes to

project delivery. Tech projects often have tight deadlines, so effective time management is essential. Techies need to prioritize tasks, set realistic goals and manage their time efficiently to meet deadlines and deliver results. Effective time management can make you make more money and make you more productive. Time management is not just an essential soft skill, but also a needed soft skill.

6. **Empathy:** Empathy involves understanding and empathizing with the perspectives, feelings, and experiences of others. In the tech industry, empathy is important for building strong relationships with colleagues, understanding user needs and designing products that meet users' requirements.

7. **Leadership:** This very important soft skill must not be overlooked. I personally believe that if you cannot lead, then you cannot expand your influence in anything. When it comes to tech, somehow you will have to lead a team of people to accomplish a task or goal. Leadership skills are valuable for tech professionals at any level, whether they are leading a team, managing projects, or influencing stakeholders. Leadership involves inspiring and motivating others, setting clear goals and expectations, making decisions

and taking responsibility for outcomes. Effective leadership will lead to accountability, collaboration and continuous improvement. Everything rises and falls on leadership.

There are many more soft skills but these are the very fundamentals that any one coming into tech need to be aware of. It will give you an edge; Soft skills play a crucial role in career advancement, professional growth and overall success in the technology industry.

Administrative Tech Skills

Administrative tech skills are skills that are related to the running of a business, organization, company and increasing productivity. Administrative tech skills are skills that are management oriented. It involves always leading a system. Administrative skills lead, manage and execute projects or tasks for companies.

These skills supervise projects in tech until they become a reality. These skills are essential for ensuring the efficient operation and maintenance of IT infrastructure, applications and services. These skills enable effective governance, operational excellence and strategic alignment of IT with business objectives. Anyone who has a proficient administrative tech skill executes any project in tech comfortably and in addition, can outsource and manage resources.

Here is a list of some well-known Administrative Tech Skill:

- **Project management:** A project manager plans, coordinates and oversees tech projects from the start to its completion. They define the scope of the project, allocate time of completion, allocate resources and ensure to deliver quality.
- **Product management:** Product Management is the process of bringing a new product to market or developing an existing one. This is one of the most high demand tech skills.
- The need to be proficient product managers, Product managers are responsible for the strategy, development and marketing of a product or service. They work closely with different teams, including engineering, design, marketing and sales, to define product features, prioritize development efforts, and deliver solutions that meet customer needs.
- While product managers may perform administrative tasks related to project management and coordination, their primary focus is on driving product vision, strategy and execution to achieve business objectives.

- **Network Administration:** Network administrators are very essential in today's world; they manage network infrastructure components and protocols, such as routers, switches, firewalls and IP addressing. This includes configuring network devices, monitoring network performance, troubleshooting and implementing security measure to protect against cyber threats.
- **System Administration:** Managing and maintaining computer systems, servers, and operating systems. This includes tasks such as installing and configuring software, applying patches and updates, monitoring system performance and troubleshooting issues to ensure optimal reliability and performance.
- **IT Asset Management**
- **Database Administration:** The Ability to administer and maintain databases, including data backup and recovery, performance tuning, user access control and database security management. Proficiency in database management systems (DBMS) such as MySQL, Oracle, or SQL Server is essential.

Administrative skills are much and we may not cover all here but if you want to understand more about these skills, you can do a personal research, Administrative tech skills are essential tech skills responsible for managing and maintaining technological infrastructure and services within an organization and companies

Marketing Tech Skills

These are tech skills used to market tech products. Tech marketing skill, also known as technology marketing, involves promoting and selling technology-related products, solutions, and services to target audiences. Tech marketers require a combination of technical knowledge, marketing expertise and digital skills to effectively reach and engage their audience.

These skills are highly needed skills. Since the tech world became open and more popular, many tech products that can solve real problems came into existence and they are constantly looking for proficient people who market their product. A tech product is not yet a product until it can sell and solve the problem for which it was bought.

Tech marketing is a very large and here are the list of some Marketing Tech skill:

1. Digital Marketing
2. Search Engine Optimization (SEO)
3. Content Marketing, Email Marketing
4. Marketing Automation
5. Social Media Marketing

6. Data Analysis and Analytics
7. Email marketing

As you may already know, having read thus far, the tech field is a very large one and what I did here is try the best I can to categorize them so that someone can gain direction just by glancing through this book.

I believe this section has helped you gain direction on how you can pick a skill. If you have come this far with me on this journey, I commend you because it shows your readiness to break into tech with ease. Let us now move into how to acquire these tech skills in the next chapter.

CHAPTER 7

WAYS TO ACQUIRE A TECH SKILL?

In a technological advanced world, tech skills can now be acquired in different ways. Acquiring a tech skill now is much easier than ever. You can read, watch, be directed or mentored by someone; the main goal is that there is a transference of tech skill information.

I will like to show you Four (4) proven ways to acquire tech skills. They include:

- University
- Paid courses online and offline too,
- Free resource
- Mentorship / Apprenticeship

Now let us take a cursory gaze at each of these methods of acquiring tech skills.

1. University

Modern day universities now offer certain tech skills as degree courses. Some universities have seen that there is a need to include these courses in the curriculum in order to produce market/ job ready students. There is now a possibility of pursuing degree in a relevant field such as computer science, information technology, engineering, or even a specialized area like data science, cybersecurity or software engineering and the likes when you learn from a university. It is called formal education.

2. Paid courses online and offline

You can acquire a tech skill by paying for a course online. A few of these online platforms include Udemy, Coursera, Skillshare etc but the issue is that you don't know for sure which course will deliver you the result you need.

Here is how to know if a course you're about to pay for will really teach you what you want;

- ➢ Reading other peoples reviews on the course is very important on any learning platform. If you see a 60% to 80% good review please go for the course, because for every 10 'yeses', there must be one 'no'. It may not be 100% perfect.
- ➢ Go through the free course, every online course at least should grant you access to the first few lessons.
- ➢ A very good course should have a good rating. Something like top-rated or bestseller or something similar. If a course is a bestseller, it did not appear

there by chance or any fraudulent means. It means the course is worth it.

- ➢ Review the curriculum if it is up-to-date. The question is how would you know if it is up to date? Do research about the tech skill you want to learn, check for the update and see if it matches the curriculum.

Taking advantage of online learning platforms such as Coursera, Udemy, edX, LinkedIn Learning, or Pluralsight to access courses, tutorials and training materials on a wide range of tech topics can make a difference in your tech journey.

3. Free resource

Once it comes to free resources YouTube comes first as a platform. In addition, yes, there are tons of free quality resources that can be found there. However, the real issue is finding them. As I will always tell my friends, YouTube is the biggest knowledge bank. It is a university on its own.

However, if you are not guided you will end up learning randomly. Let me quickly guide you on how to pick courses and good quality videos on YouTube.

Here are some keys for you:

- Look for videos that are taught in series example part 1 to part 10: Once you are looking for videos on a particular field check for videos in series
- Go to a learning platform like Udemy. get the name of the owner of the course and do a name search for it on YouTube to see if he or she has a YouTube channel. If they do, check their videos or their playlist and you may find free quality resources there.
- Get 3 Tutors on YouTube that you have become comfortable with and follow their teaching especially on a subject area they are known for (which you seek for).
- When you search for videos, make sure you pay attention to the date. Before you watch videos on any course you want to learn, let the videos be maximum of 1 year old to 6 months old anything 2 years to 3 years may not give you exactly what you need.

Remember the tech world is dynamic and constantly changing. Have that in mind when searching for videos. Therefore, search for videos based on the present year or most recent year. For example, Flutter mobile app development 2024, UI/UX 2023/2024, etc.

When you search this way, what pops up is usually quality present videos or you take Udemy course creator name type their name with the course they offer and then the year. I believe you will find this helpful.

- Spend Quality time to research and to search for videos you want
- Sometimes do not search with the course title. Now you use this when you have already started learning with YouTube. When you hear something that is not explained well or directly in that video, write it down, do not bother looking for so many videos again, type the subject matter then add the course name at the back.

For example, let us assume we are searching for 'How to create a color palette in UI/UX and 'How to create functions in flutter and dart'. This is more specific because you are already on a learning path and you only need clarification on just one or two areas.

There are other free Resource; you can still get quality videos and other learning materials.

Examples of some other free resource with quality are:

- EdX,
- LinkedIn learning
- Couseera,
- Udacity
- Microsoft learn
- Codecademy
- Freecodecamp (also on YouTube)
- Alison
- Upskill
- Skill share

How to Design and Build Your Learning Curve

When using free resources, one thing you must learn how to do is to create and build a learning path. Building your own curriculum and structuring your learning curve is important. This leads me to show you one final thing before I wrap up this chapter. That is how to design and build your learning curve.

If you are using free resources especially from YouTube, learning path might not be organized and might just be one sided. This is why many beginners get frustrated when trying to learn from resources like YouTube. The information might be of great quality, but information that is not organized and this scatters your learning curve.

We will discuss how to can organize videos and the information you get from these platforms effectively, to help build a good learning curve.

Here are a few steps on how you can structure your learning, and be effective and grow using free resource platforms: *RESEARCH, BASIC & ADVANCED* structure.

1. **RESEARCH**: For every field you want to learn, do research on that field. Now this kind of research is the one that will help you to design your learning curve. This is how you go about the research

- Go to job description of any field you want to learn on a job board
- Check for the skill requirement
- Go to another job board (e.g. jobberman, indeed and the likes) and do the same thing
- Check like 5 job boards observe keenly skill sets that are constantly repeated in the job description. Take note and write them down
- Go to google or Chat GPT and ask for example using this prompt 'I want to become a flutter developer what are things I need to know'. Read at least 3 information results you get from 3 major platforms used. This

would then lead you to the next step, which is a very important law.

- The Law of sequence: The law of sequence states that before you count number two, you need to know what number one is and before B is A. This law simply means that for every prompt used, you were given a sequence for the information you are seeking. You would definitely observe that for every article, blog, or Chat GPT prompt, the information was organized in sequence.

  This further tells you that designing and building things in order is the goal. Now take the first information you wrote down and begin to arrange them in sequence. In the end, what seems very hard for you to get becomes easy and the good news is that you can use this formula for any skill you want to learn.

2. **BASIC:** (find every BASIC information you need to know): Search for the basic information needed in that field, then follow the sequence given; do not jump on or skip anything. Always start with the basics.

3. **ADVANCED** (Once you get comfortable with using the information and skill in basic do a research on the advance information): Search for the advance information needed, then follow the sequence given, do not jump or skip anything.

- Furthermore, go to YouTube to ask for a learning path in that field and you may see a good video that will give you a clear and direct learning path.
- Ask someone who has the experience in the skill you want to learn for assistance.

How to Sustain Your Passion to Learn and Finish Successfully

Having learned how to create a learning path, there is yet another question and it is the question of how to finish learning a free resource successfully.

Now that you have access to this valuable information, there is one more thing you need to know as someone who is just beginning to learn online, especially using free resources. You will lose your passion easily, because it costs you nothing to have access to this information other than your data. The tendency to lose your passion does exist.

You need to understand that motivation begins the journey, but it takes discipline keeps you going on your tech-learning path. You must incorporate discipline for you to succeed.

However, it is only when you decide to be disciplined that you can actually take up a free resource and stay with it until the end. So then, how do you sustain this passion and learn successfully until the end.

Here is a few helpful tips that can help:

- Remember the reason you wanted to learn a tech skill. Always remind yourself why you should continue.
- Discipline: Remember that motivation begins the journey, but discipline keeps you going.
- Burn the bridge of alternatives: This means you should try to see no other alternative than that path you have chosen to follow.
- Move beyond passion: Passion is good. However, your personal decision to continue learning is better.
- Turn your passion to goals and strive to achieve them
- Invest enough energy and time so much that you see no reason to back down.
- Focus on the result: This is placing before you what you would become after learning this skill, potential financial reward and the picture of the life you want to have based on the skill you want to acquire. These and more should remain your focus.
- Passion does not really die. If this happens, it means you have stopped feeding it. Endeavour to feed your passion with its demands. As for tech, feed it with time, energy, practice and mentorship.

Keys to Finishing What You Started In Tech

Now when learning a tech skill in order for you to finish what you started, you must know the following:

- **Start with the simple stuff:** This is where many fail. They just jump up and not grow up. When learning a tech skill, stop attempting too much. Attempt as much as you can do per time and do not overwhelm yourself with learning.

  Take it systematic because small steps repeated consistently every day lead to great achievement. When you rush to attempt too much and too soon, you are almost guaranteed to fall short of your desired result. The secret of learning anything and sustaining momentum is to start with small, simpler stuff.

- **Be patient:** Do not expect everything you try to learn to enter your head immediately. Give it time and be patient. It might be hard at first, but it would be easy as times go on.

  When you begin to learn, you might not get it immediately but the truth is you must allow patience to display to you how far you have to learn. In my experience, I found out that patience reveals how far you have grown over time. Some people never realize how close they are to achieving significant things because they give up too soon, everything worthwhile in life takes dedication and time and tech is no different.

The people who grow and achieve the most are the ones who harness the power of patience. As I have told you before, the tech industry knows how to reward patience.

- **Value the process:** One of the best things you can do for yourself as someone learning is to cultivate the ability to value and enjoy the process because most times after learning comes the process. The process of becoming (the process of growth), is where the real 'tech bros' are made.

  You will never get it immediately and the process should not be skipped. It is what sharpens and increases your skill for the marketplace. Process always pays off, anybody you see doing well in tech went through the process.

- **Plan your growth and keep improving:** Give room for improvement no matter how much progress you make. Make sure you feed your passion and do not let it die.

CHAPTER 8

NAVIGATING THE JOB MARKET

I believe this chapter is the one you have been waiting for, because here, we would be talking about money. Believe me, your journey in tech will not be exciting if you are not solving problems and making money at the same time. So long as you are solving problems in tech, your joy becomes full when your skill makes money for you.

Financial reward is a major motivation for acquiring tech skills and solving problems. Unfortunately, many have the skill but cannot use it in the marketplace, some are getting frustrated and it looks as if there is a roadblock somewhere- one that refuses to allow them to get into the market and make money.

Building Yourself for the Tech Job Market
You cannot navigate the job market if you have not dealt with certain things. The job market is a busy one and it is highly competitive. You would have to deal with certain traits and mindset in order for you to be ready to get that dream job.

Firstly, before you can thrive in tech job market, you need to equip yourself with adequate knowledge needed in your skill.

You would not want to get a bad reputation because your delivery was bad, would you? The basic is very important for you to learn. You can then think of going into the market place.

Secondly, you need to fight imposter syndrome. In Chapter 2 of this course, we have discussed extensively what imposter syndrome in tech is and how you can overcome it as you journey into tech. If not, you keep on doubting your ability and confidence, even though you have acquired so much knowledge and completed various projects.

The tech field responds to confidence as much as it does to competence. Tech beginners usually ask when the right time to apply for a job is. My answer is very simple; when you have learned the basics, done projects with it and when your courage or confidence is ready.

Individuals experiencing imposter syndrome may struggle with self-confidence, self-promotion and taking risks in their career pursuits. That feeling of 'I cannot' will likely stop you from taking that step that would land you that job.

The best way to deal with the imposter syndrome is to take a step and while taking that step ignore your fears. Personally, this is part of how I dealt with it. I just take a step not minding my fears and I keep telling myself to try it and see the outcome. Moreover, sometimes, outcomes may be good or bad but the goal is to keep taking steps.

Applying for that job and not minding the outcome and taking baby steps is what makes a giant eventually in tech. In dealing with this syndrome, Building internal confidence is key. Stop waiting for people to validate your skill or craft rather build internal confidence by believing in yourself. Self-belief is the greatest of your strengths.

You have to learn how to draw strength from within you. Learn to tell yourself continuously that you can. You can repeat it as much as 50 times and doing this every day is one way you build confidence.

Step out, after dealing with imposter syndrome, step out and apply for that job. Share your craft and make noise with it. Let people know what you are doing. No matter how good you are, if someone does not know you exist, it is the same as not having a skill at all. Most importantly, when applying for jobs, see failure and rejection as part of the process.

Finally, you are ready for work! After equipping yourself with the needed knowledge, stepping out boldly by overcoming imposter syndrome, you need to craft a stand-out tech resume. Here, I am not just talking about a 'standard' resume but a 'stand-out' resume. This cannot be overemphasized.

Your resume displays your worth and your skill. Before an employer gets to hire you, he/she meets you first with your resume.

Your resume is actually you on paper or electronic form. Crafting a standout tech resume means creating a resume that effectively showcases your technical skills, experience and accomplishments in a way that makes you stand out to potential employers.

There are key elements that you need to include for it to become a standout resume, here are a few:

- Let your resume be clear, clean and have a professional layout with clear heading and bullet point. These things make your resume easy to read and navigate as well as avoid excesses on it.
- Let your resume for each job application highlight the most relevant skills, experience. If you do not have real world experience, state your personal project. Tailor your resume to show that you understand the role and are genuinely interested in the position.
- Let your resume be easily understood- Keep it simple
- Show your relevant work experience- relevant work experiences, internships, projects or personal initiative

that demonstrates your technical abilities and problem solving skills.
- Proofread your resume carefully for grammatical and spelling errors and let your formatting and styling be consistent throughout. Pay attention to details. Attention to detail is crucial in the tech industry and a flawless resume can make a positive impression on recruiters.
- Let your resume be visually appealing- A visually appealing resume can also help you stand out.
- Let your resume effectively communicate your technical expertise.

As you start applying for jobs, don't forget to link your resume to your portfolio. A portfolio is a collection of work samples, projects, or accomplishments that showcase an individual's skills, experiences and expertise in a particular field. In the context of a tech resume, a portfolio often includes examples of software projects, coding samples, designs, case studies or other relevant work that demonstrates proficiency and capabilities.

A tech portfolio can be an effective tool for job seekers to supplement their resume and provide concrete evidence of their abilities to potential employers. It allows candidates to showcase their problem-solving skills, creativity and technical proficiency in a tangible and visually appealing way.

Additionally, a portfolio can help candidates differentiate themselves from other applicants and make a stronger impression during the hiring process. When creating a tech portfolio, it is essential to choose relevant and high-quality examples of your work, provide context or explanations where necessary and ensure that the portfolio is well-organized and easy to navigate.

Depending on the nature of the work samples, a tech portfolio can be presented in various formats - such as a website, PDF document or online portfolio platform. (Like Behance, Dribble , GitHub , many times a personal website)

Actually, you need to apply more when hunting for job, especially remote jobs. It is a number game and a long-term game. Don't expect a nice reply and don't expect a yes immediately, but flow with the process.

Apart from applying for jobs either remotely or physically, there are other ways to get jobs or to market your skills. Job is very good; it is secure and it can come with other benefits.

What if you have tried without getting positive results when applying for jobs in their numbers? There is another means of selling your skill or giving yourself jobs. It is called Freelancing.

Introduction to Freelancing?

Freelancing refers to working as an independent contractor or self-employed individual, typically offering services or skills to clients on a project basis. Freelancers are not typically bound to a single employer for a long-term and have the flexibility to work with multiple clients on various projects simultaneously.

It is any legitimate type of work done online for which you get paid, from graphic designing to web designing, social media marketing, writing, customer service, programming as well as many others.

Freelancing is one of the easiest ways to break into tech especially if you have been applying for jobs for a very long time and you know your skills are worth it, try selling your skill as an independent contractor. Employ yourself with your skill, rather than waiting for a company to pay you a certain amount monthly.

With freelancing, you can earn even more, but I must warn you; you must be willing to put in the work, because this is you building your personal business. You are not just selling a skill, but you are doing real business.

Freelancers are considered to be self-employed and are responsible for managing their own business affairs including invoicing, clients, paying taxes and securing their own insurance and many more. Simply put, you can take freelancing as being your own boss.

They have the freedom to set their own schedules, choose their clients and projects and work from anywhere with an internet connection. The best part of freelancing I like is that you get to work for different people, different clients, experience different projects and get to learn new things, as it is very flexible.

It offers flexibility in terms of workload and working hours, allowing you to balance work with personal commitments or pursue other interests. Because of the nature of freelancing, I would encourage you, as a tech newbie, to start with freelancing. Most of the time it is the fastest way to break into tech, grow and even build a business. Freelancing will give you the exposure you need to thrive and grow in tech.

Freelancers often work on a diverse range of projects for different clients, which can provide exposure to various industries, challenges and opportunities for professional growth.

How to Get Freelancing Gigs/Contract

There are many ways to get freelancing gigs but I would be focusing on just two of them.

These two formats are:

- Leveraging on freelancing platform
- Using social media as a freelancing platform

We will discuss extensively on these two methods and you can always choose the best for you to land gigs in your tech skills.

1. Leveraging on Freelancing Platforms

There are many freelancing platforms out there and one must know how to use them properly. Here are some useful information you need to pay attention to when learning how to use a freelancing platform:

> **Choose the right platform:** Research and compare different freelancing platforms to find one that best suits your skills, expertise and preferences. Some popular freelancing platforms include Upwork, Freelancer, Fiverr, Guru and Toptal. Consider factors such as the types of projects available and fee structures. Once you choose a freelancing platform try to study and understand the platform and how best to use it.

- **Create a profile:** Sign up for an account on the chosen freelancing platform and complete your profile. Your profile is your digital resume for clients to access you. You should highlight your skills, experience, portfolio and any relevant certifications or qualifications.

  Use a professional photo and write a compelling bio that highlights your expertise and attracts potential clients. Your profile is the first thing your potential clients see before reaching out to you. An optimized profile on any of the freelancing platforms mentioned above is what makes you attract clients.

- **Set Your Rates:** Determine your pricing structure based on factors such as your skill level, experience, market demand and competition. Do a Research on what other freelancers in your field are charging on the platform and adjust your rates accordingly.

  Consider offering different pricing options, such as hourly rates, fixed-price packages, or retainer agreements. However, as a newbie or beginner in any of this platform I would advise you start with the lowest rate and then build up from there. This advice would help you land jobs quickly then you start growing on the platform.

- **Create a Portfolio:** Build a portfolio displaying your past work, projects and achievements. Include samples of your work, case studies, client testimonials and any other relevant information that demonstrates your skills and expertise. A strong portfolio helps potential clients evaluate your capabilities before making hiring decisions.
- **Search for Jobs:** Browse for jobs on the freelancing platform and filter them based on your skills, preferences and availability. Look for projects that match your expertise and interests and carefully read the job descriptions, requirements and client reviews before submitting proposals.
- **Submit Proposals:** Write proposals tailored to the job description, addressing the client's specific needs, challenges and project requirements. Highlight your relevant experiences, skills, and how you can add value to the client's project. Customize each proposal to demonstrate your understanding of the client's needs and showcase why you are the best fit for the job.
- **Communicate Professionally:** Maintain clear and professional communication with clients throughout the hiring process. Respond promptly to messages, ask clarifying questions and provide updates on your

progress. Building a positive rapport with clients can lead to long-term relationships and repeat business. Always sustain a positive energy. This reminds me of my clients who always add to my review: 'I love your energy.'

- **Manage Finances and Contracts:** Keep track of your earnings, expenses and invoices using accounting software or spreadsheets. Negotiate clear contracts or agreements with clients outlining project scope, deliverables, timelines, payment terms, and any other relevant terms and conditions. Ensure that both parties understand and agree to the terms before starting work.
- **Seek Feedback and Improve:** After completing projects, ask clients for feedback and testimonials to showcase on your profile. Use constructive criticism to identify areas for improvement and continuously refine your skills, processes and service offerings. Learning from client feedback helps you grow as a freelancer and build a strong reputation in the freelancing community.

If you follow these steps and actively participate in these freelancing platforms, you can learn how to effectively use these platforms to find clients, secure projects and build a successful freelancing business. If you master the act of freelancing you will not only break into tech; you will never go hungry because for every time someone needs your skill, you make money freelancing service base. I urge you to go and sell your skill and be your boss. Money made from the freelancing world is called the gig economy.

2. Using Social Media As A Freelancing Platform

Social media is not just a platform for fun but also a marketplace for your craft. Every social media platform is a marketing tool. So long as you have an audience and people are using that platform, that's a marketplace. People actually make up the market and anywhere you find people, you can market your skill. Someone will most likely need your skill.

Using social media as a freelancing platform can be an effective strategy for finding clients, promoting your services and building your brand as a freelancer. Identify which social media platforms are most relevant to your target audience and industry. For professional freelancers, platforms like LinkedIn, Twitter and Facebook are commonly used for networking, showcasing expertise and finding clients.

To harness these platforms, you need to create professional profiles on the chosen social media platforms, ensuring consistency in branding, messaging and imagery. Use a high-quality profile photo and write a compelling bio that highlights your skills, expertise and services. Do not fail to include relevant keywords and hashtags in your profile to improve visibility and searchability.

Share relevant and engaging content that showcases your expertise, educates your audience and provides value. This could include tips, tutorials, case studies, portfolio samples, industry insights or success stories. Use different forms such as text, images, videos, and infographics to keep your content diverse and engaging.

As you post, actively engage your audience by responding to comments, messages and inquiries on time. Learn to also participate in relevant discussions, join industry-related groups and communities and network with potential clients and collaborators

Use social media to promote your freelance services and offerings. Share updates about your availability, new projects, client testimonial and special promotions or discounts. Create eye-catching graphics or videos to showcase your work and attract attention to your services.

Collaborate with other freelancers, influencers, or businesses in complementary industries to expand your reach and attract new clients. Track and analyze your social media performance using built-in analytics tools or third-party analytics platforms. Monitor key metrics such as engagement, reach, click-through rates, and conversions to assess the effectiveness of your social media effort.

Consistency is key when using social media as a freelancing platform. Post regularly, maintain a consistent brand voice and aesthetic, stay active, and engaged with your audience. Building a presence and reputation on social media takes time and effort, so be patient and persistent in your efforts.

In the next Chapter, you will learn how to create content and post them on social media platforms, because content is king when it comes to social media freelancing.

CHAPTER 9

Maximizing Social media Platforms as a Freelancer

How to Create and Post Content on Social Media Platforms

In the previous chapter, we discussed how you could leverage on social media platforms to showcase your expertise, we will discuss more on how you can create irresistible content position yourself on social media platforms.

In order to maximize your social media platforms as a freelancer, there are some secrets I would like to share with you. These secrets are as follows:

1. Understand the struggles of people or the potential client you are looking to serve.

- What are they struggling with the most?
- Why haven't they been able to solve their problems yet?
- What is a major roadblock holding them back from achieving success?
- What are their biggest fears and pain points?
- Why do they need help right now?

2. Create Solutions to their Problems

- How do your skills/services help them achieve their desired outcome?
- How can you remove their pain points and deliver them to their goals?
- What specific solutions do you have that can help them solve their problems right now?
- How long will it take you to do it?
- What is the value in you doing it? How urgent is it?

3. Create your offer

- Your offer comes before content, outreach, fulfillment, and everything else.
- Nothing matters if you don't have an offer that people WANT & NEED.
- There needs to be an actual demand for what you're selling, but you also need to position your offer in a way that stands out from the crowd.
- Never try to create an offer that you just think people will want. Create what you know people will want.

Creating an In-Demand Offer

Now here's how to craft an in demand, no-brainer offer:

- Test Market Demand: Understand what's in demand within your niche. What are your target market's biggest pain points?
- Make it a No-Brainer. Establish your uniqueness with what you offer.
- Put yourself in the buyer's shoes and ask yourself some crucial questions. Questions may include the following: Would I buy what I'm selling? If your answer isn't a guaranteed 'yes', then you have some thinking to do. With this question in mind, think of the elements you could add or subtract that would align more with the market's demands and make your offer a complete no-brainer and better than anything else in the market.
- Consider your positioning. Equally as important to your offer is your positioning. Positioning is what will place you at a vantage point and keep you ahead of your competitors. It will prevent you from being just another tech guy randomly looking for clients.

How do you uniquely position yourself?

To position yourself, you must do to understand your unique selling proposition. What's the reason customers buy from you in the first place and who is your perfect customer? Your unique selling proposition will differentiate you from competitors. It's the reason people choose you over others even if they have 10 similar offers.

Therefore, you need to ask yourself these questions; how can I show the unique selling point of my offer via my content? This is because unique mechanisms create unique results. The way you approach solving your clients' problems will affect the results you get for them. Taking a unique approach means you can generate results that others don't have. You can leverage these results and incorporate them into your brand's positioning.

You need to communicate your uniqueness in such a way that your client would see you differently and would be ready to do business with you.

Consider this template below for example (You can use this template as guide for yours):

"I've generated [unique results] for my clients through [a unique process], and I can do the same for you as well".

Your unique mechanism creates your unique results.

Social Media Client Acquisition Funnel

The Purpose of all content marketing is to build trust with the audience by demonstrating that you know what you're talking about. It's all about the confidence with which you reveal your competence. People want to be sure you really know what you are doing.

In today's social media driven world, the first point of contact between you and a potential customer is when they land on your social media profile or any of your social media platforms.

You need to stay on "brand" with what your profile portrays but also add a splash of personality. Nobody likes a boring dude. Make it interesting as people meet you without downplaying your competence.

1. **Your Social Media Profile**

Now let us speak about your profile and explain exactly what your profile should look like. There are essential ingredients in your profile and you must pay attention to it.

Here is a few (though from a more general point of view):

Name: Have your service / function as your name.

Bio: Let your profile have good details of you. It should answer the following questions:

- Where are you now?
- Where have you been? That is, where you are coming from.
- What are you doing to reach your goal?
- What are you learning?
- What are you building?
- How are the things you are learning and building going to help others achieve the same goal as yours? Your goal is unique to you and others can have the same goal but a different way of getting there. Your path should serve as a guiding light and source of inspiration for others.

Take some time to answer all of these questions, as that would give you firepower to create a more authentic bio for yourself.

Banner or Cover Photo: It should reinforce the text in your bio. Something simple is most effective. Use benefit driven text with appealing aesthetics.

Profile Picture: Use a clear headshot picture to build trust.

2. How to Post Your Content

Now you need to know about content posting, which is another aspect of social media building and it's used in creating awareness about your brand, business, services, etc.

The function of social media is to be social and connect with people. The truth is that I can give you a formula but at the end of the day, if you're not saying anything interesting (while making content), giving any value or teaching people things, you will not get followers regardless of how much engagement you have. I would advise you to focus on twitter and LinkedIn. These platforms are among the big ones. They are like gold mines.

Now I need to show you how you can grow your followership on social media through your content and engagement. The following represents different categories based on followership and how you can grow into each level. At each level, I will be sharing insights on how to grow at each level.

Level 1: 0 - 500 followers

- At least 2 posts per day on any social media platform you are using.

    One very good, information given and valuable post or thread pinned on your profile can make a difference.

- At least 15 comments on other accounts per day. These comments CANNOT just be 'rewording' of what somebody has already said. You must inject your own

anecdotes, unique experience, or ADD to what they said.
- Respond to every single comment you get on your own tweets.
- Respond to every single DM you get
- Outbound comments to 10% accounts with above 10k followers, 50% account with 3000 to 10,000 followers, and 60% to accounts with below 3,000 followers

Level 2: 500 - 1000 followers

- At least 2 post or tweet per day
- At least 1 thread on twitter and 1 article on LinkedIn per week, repost on any other social media platform
- At least 10 comments on other accounts per day
- Respond to every single comment you get
- Respond to every single DM you get
- Outbound comments to 10% accounts with above 10k followers, 50% accounts with 3000 to 10,000 followers and 60% to accounts with below 3,000 followers.

Level 3: 1000 - 3000 followers

- At least 3 post or tweet per day
- At least 1 thread on twitter and 1 article on LinkedIn per week , repost on any other social media platform

- At least 10 comments on other accounts per day
- Respond to every single comment you get
- Respond to every single DM you get
- Outbound comments to 10% accounts with above 10k followers, 50% account with 3000 to 10,000 followers, and 60% to accounts with below 3,000 followers

Level 4: 3000 - 10000 followers

- At least 3 post or tweet per day
- At least 1 thread on twitter and 1 article on LinkedIn per week , repost on any other social media platform
- At least 10 comments on other accounts per day
- Respond to every single comment you get
- Respond to every single DM you get
- Outbound comments to 30% accounts with above 10k followers, 60% 10,000-3,000, 10% below 3,000, these numbers do not have to be exactly precise but will give you a great guideline on what works.

3. **Creating A Posting Time Table/Schedule**

The following can serve as a guide to helping you create your weekly posting schedule:

Monday: 1 thread and article, 2 tweets and post,

Tuesday: 1 teaching, 1 tweet and post,

Wednesday: 2 tweets and post, 1 question and answer

Thursday: 1 thread and article, 2 tweets and post

Friday: 1 mind map, 1 question 1 tweet and post

Saturday: 2 tweets and post, 1 thread and 1 article

Sunday: 1 question and answer, 1 tweet and post,

The general rule follows:

- If you have below 1,000 followers, tweeting and posting more will not get you more followers because there's nobody to see your tweets or post
- If you have below 1,000 followers the biggest driving factor is the amount of outbound comments you're making

As you grow followers, the amount of tweets and post you put out becomes increasingly more important, and outbound comments become less important

Responding to all comments will push your back onto the timeline of your followers who are actively on that social media platform (do not underestimate this. You MUST do this).

NB: As a way of balance, you must understand that there are no hard or fast rules to this.

Sometimes things may not always go by the book. The process may not follow in this order but you can achieve the result. The key is finding the right method that works for you.

This is a guide that can help you fast track your progress.

The term 'DM' actually refers to Direct Messages received in your personal inbox on any social media platform. In addition, the term 'Tweet' refers to posts made on the X (formerly twitter) social media platform.

CHAPTER 10

TECH MENTOR

In general, Mentorship is a dynamic relationship between two individual, where one person (the mentor) share his or her knowledge and experiences to support the growth and development of the other person (the mentee. If you want to go far in any field, not just in tech, you need a mentor.

A knowledge-based techie will never outsmart an experienced-based techie. That is why you need a mentor. You need someone to tell you about the journey and guide you in the path you are about to go through.

The goal of mentorship is to involve guidance, advice, feedback and encouragement; all aimed at helping the mentee achieve their personal and professional goals. Mentors were once in your position, some had guidance and some did not. Moreover, most importantly, they made mistakes they can help avoid.

Who is a Tech Mentor?
A Tech mentor is one who is involved and helping other people rise in tech. It is a relationship between an experienced tech professional who is the mentor and a less experienced

individual, the mentee in the field of tech. Mentors are there to provide guidance, support and useful advice that would help in the skill and character development of the mentee.

Why do you need a Mentor?

A tech mentor is important in tech. In my opinion, I would say that it is the fastest route to learning and solidifying your knowledge in that skill. Mentors can see where you are going even before you see it and help you arrive there on time if you would just listen and follow.

You need a tech mentor because many struggle for a long time before standing in the tech field just because they did not have any guidance. Mentors shorten your journey. What would have taken you time to achieve, just by having a mentor and listening to them, your journey can be short.

Mentorship is one factor that should not be ignored in tech. If you take mentorship seriously, you will forever be one step ahead of your peers in any field. Therefore, I encourage you to submit yourself to mentorship.

Do bear in mind that mentorship is not just listening to a man but mentorship is submitting yourself to build the character, trait, habit and principles of a man. The secret of any successful man is found in his mentorship. You can become anything if you find a reference. Mentorship involves buying into the idea and thought process of a man.

Do not just be an excited follower: be a follower who takes in information and knowledge from your mentor very seriously. Listen to the stories of your mentors; their secret is found in their stories. Understand the mindset of your mentor, believe and live by the principle you learn from your mentor.

Let me quickly add that if you must follow a mentor, you must believe in your mentor. If you don't believe in your mentor, don't follow. Follow who you want to be like, follow people you believe in. Believing is the seed for receiving. Mentors have secrets and they are looking for who to share with if only you can listen.

When you come before a mentor, try as much as you can to forget that you know something, forget about your past result. Your results most times are useless before a mentor because he has many times over what you call an achievement. Focus on your goals and why you are seeking mentorship. Whatever you saw in that fellow that made you desire to follow them, that should be your goal, focus on it.

In mentorship, learn to be observant. When following a mentor, do not expect him to tell you everything. The truth is that there are things in mentorship that can only be gotten by observation. In mentorship, some things are taught and many others are caught by keen observation. There are things mentors may not remember to tell you but your observation will give you that answer.

Be a highly focused and purpose driven person when following a mentor. Focus is what makes you learn quickly and observe accurately. Actually, focus can bring you closer to your mentor especially if it is a long distance mentorship. Every time you enter the presence of a mentor, learn to be focused, and very observant.

Take note of this fact as you begin to follow with focus and high degree observation, you will notice that you will start becoming and looking like your mentor and inadvertently, you will start experiencing their results.

There is a mistake many people make when it comes to mentorship. This is the mistake of disconnecting from a mentor. Never disconnect from your mentor; remain connected. Yes, a time can come in your journey when you feel like you don't need them again. Well, be careful because this is where many great people fail.

No matter how tall a skyscraper is, it will remain standing so long as it is still connected to the ground. There is no floating skyscraper. Every skyscraper has a foundation. There is no skyscraper that becomes so tall and begins to touch the clouds and then disconnects itself from the ground. It won't last for long before crumbling into debris. That is how mentorship is.

Mentors are your foundation. You are building and standing on mentorship. Most times, you are not ready for the real world, because you have no mentor. My dear friend, you need a tech mentor. You need someone in tech to help you navigate your way in the tech industry.

Mentoring is so important because of the impact it has on people's lives. Studies have shown that when adults mentor young people, there is an effect on their ability to prevent and delay declining brain function. There is something about mentoring that makes you feel good and safe. Mentoring makes you ready for the future.

Types of Mentor

There are two kinds of mentors you will meet in life; Intentional Mentors and Unintentional Mentors.

- International Mentors constantly seek opportunities to help others grow and achieve great things.
- Unintentional Mentors are the kind of people that are mentors without even knowing that they are mentors. They can influence your life and you don't even know that you're already being mentored by them.

I have had many mentors in my life both intentional mentors and unintentional mentors.

They have all helped me to grow in various aspects of my life and my tech career. My simple advice for you is this; never work alone in tech. You need someone who has gone ahead of you, who has crossed that river you are about to cross so many times.

There is a big difference between mentors and role models. Mentors have the ability to lead in every situation. Mentors help you see what you cannot see in yourself. One day of mentoring can change your life forever. Get a tech mentor today. Mentorship can eliminate your fear and doubt.

Benefit of a Tech Mentor
1. Mentors offer valuable insights, guidance and advice based on their own experiences in the tech field. They help mentees overcome challenges, make the right decisions and overcome obstacles in their career development.
2. Mentors help mentees expand their network and make valuable connections within the tech community. They may introduce mentees to other techies, provide networking opportunities and introduce them to potential employers or collaborators.

3. Mentors help mentees in developing technical skills, soft skills and outstanding competencies relevant to their role and career goals.
4. Mentors serve as role models for mentees. They help you see who you can become and what you can become as you grow.

How to Get Access to Mentors?
1. Use online platforms to access mentorship. Platforms like LinkedIn can help. You can connect with experienced professionals who are willing to mentor others.
2. Attend tech conferences, meetups, workshops and networking events both online and offline.
3. Tech event provide you with opportunities to meet industry professionals and get connected and gain access to potential mentors who share same interests and goal

Your mentor should be accessible. You should be able to reach out to him or her, and he or she should give you a response. Mentorship is not complete until you can get feedback from your mentor.

How to Follow Mentors
1. Recognize that Mentors are not necessarily your friend. Don't expect them to always smile with you. When following your mentors, always see them as mentors and focus on the goals which is to learn and allow the transfer of knowledge.
2. Expect a mentor to stretch you. Mentors want you to grow so no matter how they stretch you it is for your good.
3. Do not be a burden to your mentor, meaning when you drop a question allow them to answer you in their time.
4. Follow them on social media, read their posts and repost.
5. Attend their events offline and online.
6. Try reaching out to them in a humble and polite manner. Remember, they have their lives to live and you are not the only one in the picture.
7. Mentors are smart, don't try to teach them. Don't come as an arrogant and unteachable person. Instead, have a teachable mind and spirit. Mentors give all they know to people willing to listen.

CHAPTER 11

TECH ADVICE

If you have read this amazing book from the very first Chapter until now, I must salute your tenacity and dogged commitment to transformation. It's incredible and I'm excited about your progress and the breakthrough that awaits you in the tech industry. You are one of a kind and your success story will be told someday. In fact, very soon!

The information I am about to share with you in this chapter was obtained from my experience. It's simply advice from my tech journey. Nothing is as inspiring as a story that brings hope and inspiration. That's why I tagged this chapter ***Tech Advice.***

My Tech Advices for You

The advice I am about to share with you stems from my own experience in the tech space. I believe it holds wisdom for you but it's not exhaustive of all that there is. It's advice based on my personal experience and you could glean valuable lessons from them for your own journey.

I will like to share with you great tips from my experiences, as you aspire to begin your journey into tech space and here are a few pieces of advice that I believe will be of great help to you:

Advice 1 - Be Single

When you begin your tech journey, you could start with one skill but you may not continue with that one skill. You will need more than that which you started with. This is my first tech advice.

If you want to go far in tech, especially as a newbie, focus on one skill until you become proficient. This is why I captioned this as 'Be Single'. Let your whole attention and energy be directed to one skill, to the point where even in your sleep you can defend that skill.

The mistake I made when I first got into the tech industry was that I did not get a good grasp yet in a skill before I started learning another one. It took me time to be proficient in all and if I were to start tech from the beginning, I would spend a lot of time mastering that one tech skill before moving to another skill. I would say 'be single before multiplication' because it helps you have a solid foundation in tech. Focus on one skill per time. Never forget this.

Advice 2 - Multiply

After you must have become good at a skill, then you can multiply. You can add any other skill, however, don't just add any skill. How do you add skills? Add skills that complement the other skills you already have. For example, I am a mobile app and web developer. I added UI/UX design to my skill to complement the design aspect of my original skill.

When skills complement each other it almost looks as if you have one skill but indirectly, you have multiple skills that can work with each other. As I advanced in my career, I added product management.

Why add product management? Since, I develop Mobile apps, websites and I am a designer, I can now manage the design and development to achieve a project. If you can successfully multiply, you are at advantage because multiple skills are equal to multiple opportunities.

Advice 3 - Self Assessment/Goal Setting

As you advance in your career there is a need for self-assessment. Try to make sure that you do a recheck on your skill. Check for updates, do a recheck on your skill level, check if you are using an updated pattern in your projects, recheck the success of your client and other projects. When you do a self-assessment as a techie, you are setting yourself up for success. It helps you know what to work on.

Self-assessment in tech involves evaluating your tech skills, knowledge as well as identifying strengths, weaknesses and areas for improvement within the field of technology. Conducting a self-assessment is important for identifying gaps in your knowledge.

Self-assessment leads to setting goals for professional development and determining your readiness for specific roles or projects. Plan to upgrade yourself using the information received from your self-assessment.

Advice 4 - Create a Long Term Career Plan

Don't come into tech to do business for a short time; have a long term vision. Having a long term vision is what keeps you going, keeps you growing, setting clear goals and identifying opportunities for your growth and development. This will lead to career advancement and longevity in tech.

Advice 5 - Learn To Overcome Challenges in Tech

Being a techie has its own challenges and for you to overcome challenges in the tech industry, it would require stamina, resilience, adaptability and proactiveness. They are highly needed when solving problems. Challenges will come but it is your job to overcome them. They are not meant to win you; you are meant to overcome them.

The way to overcome challenges when you meet them in your tech journey are by doing the following:

- Staying curious and enjoy learning: Make sure you embrace a growth mindset and see challenges as opportunities for learning and growing. Let your desire for knowledge never die.
- Seek support: Never hesitate to seek support and guidance from colleagues and mentors. The internet is your friend. Use it to your advantage.
- Stay positive and maintain a solution-oriented mindset. Focus on finding solutions rather than dwelling on problems. Challenges are not forever. They always have solutions.
- Take some time to sleep: Once you wake up, go back and face that challenge again. Try not to be overwhelmed and anxious to solve the problem; try relaxing a bit. Give yourself a break.
- Learn from your current challenges because you will need them to solve another problem.
- By developing your own unique strategies and approaches. It can help you solve problems faster and

much easier. Develop resistance and problem solving skills needed to overcome challenges and grow in tech.

Future Proofing Your Tech Career

Money is good in tech but an up-to-date tech skill is better. The best way to future-proof your career in tech is to stay up to date. Sustain a high learning ability by staying current with industrial trends.

You can future proof your tech career by applying the following advice:

- By having a high desire to keep learning. If you continue to learn and apply what you know, you will be at the forefront of your career.
- Take personal development very seriously.
- Take a break in order to relearn or learn new things. Did you know that if you take out 40 days once or twice in a year to focus on learning something you will be among the top 5 in your field? Think about that for a moment and make good use of this information.
- The power of mentorship. Mentorship is powerful in building and shaping you into a great future. You can check the previous chapter to know how mentors can help you on your tech journey.

CONCLUSION

I would like to end with a few words of encouragement and caution in order to help you strike a favorable balance between work and life. Many people don't realize that breaking into tech may lead to shortcomings on their part if not managed properly. If you are carried away by the successes that come from breaking into tech, then they can become detrimental to your life. That's why you need to pay close attention to these few words as you come to the end of this book.

The moment you break into tech and you begin to work and handle different jobs, as full time 9 to 5 or as a freelancer, please take care of your health. Like the popular saying, *'health is wealth'*. Take care of yourself, sleep when you need to sleep and rest well. As you allocate different times for work and personal development, plan your rest season as well. This advice is mostly for freelancers, especially those who take many jobs at the same time. Take care of your health.

Many tech roles require long hours of sitting in front of a computer screen, leading to a sedentary lifestyle. Prolonged sitting has been linked to various health issues including obesity, cardiovascular disease and others. Take some time off to exercise your body.

Constant exposure to screens can lead to eyestrain, headaches and digital fatigue. Techies may experience symptoms such as dry eyes, blurred vision and difficulty focusing which can negatively affect your productivity and overall well-being.

For some persons, I'll advise you get special screen glasses. The demanding nature of the tech industry can contribute to high stress levels among techies. Tight deadlines, project pressures, and frequent changes can lead to chronic stress, anxiety and burnout if not managed effectively.

Learn to manage your stress. By prioritizing health and well-being, techies can improve their quality of life, enhance their productivity and performance and sustain long-term success in their careers.

If I may add, prioritize your family. Nobody needs you as much as your family even as you strive to become better and productive in the tech industry.

Create time for your family. If you are married, create time for your spouse as well as your children. If anything happens to you on the job, your family will be worse hit compared to your boss.

You can be replaced on the job in 24 hours but your family cannot replace you even in 24 years. Your family needs you and a major part of why you are working is for them. Do not forget this as you break into the tech industry.

The Sky is Just the Beginning – **GO and Break into the Tech Industry!**

www.ingramcontent.com/pod-product-compliance
Lightning Source LLC
Chambersburg PA
CBHW050259230526
45471CB00005B/1946